KANSAS CITY
CHRONICLES

KANSAS CITY
CHRONICLES

AN UP-TO-DATE HISTORY

DAVID W. JACKSON

THE
History
PRESS

Published by The History Press
Charleston, SC 29403
www.historypress.net

First published 2010

ISBN 978.1.5402.0479.0

Library of Congress Cataloging-in-Publication Data

Jackson, David W., 1969-
Kansas City chronicles : an up-to-date history / David Jackson.
p. cm.
Includes index.
ISBN 978-1-59629-986-3
1. Kansas City (Mo.)--History. 2. Kansas City (Mo.)--Biography. 3. Kansas City (Mo.)-
-Social life and customs. 4. Historic buildings--Missouri--Kansas City. 5. Kansas City
(Mo.)--Buildings, structures, etc. 6. Kansas City Region (Mo.)--History. 7. Jackson County
(Mo.)--History. 8. Jackson County (Mo.)--History, Local. 9. Historic buildings--Missouri--
Jackson County. I. Title.
F474.K257J33 2010
977.8'411--dc22
2010019854

Notice: The information in this book is true and complete to the best of our knowledge. It is
offered without guarantee on the part of the author or The History Press. The author and
The History Press disclaim all liability in connection with the use of this book.

Contents

CONTENTS

CONTENTS

INTRODUCTION

Pulitzer Prize–winning historian and author David McCullough said of Jackson County (which encompasses Kansas City south of the Missouri River), "I can't think of another piece of landscape of similar size where so many things have happened that have been of significance in the story of America." This is a small selection of stories relaying some of the highlights that make the Kansas City metropolitan area's heritage unique to American history.

To reinforce my position that much history transpires in less than one person's lifetime, the vignettes presented here are generally grouped in 50-year increments. They cover more than 175 years of local history and include the time *before* Jackson County was formed in 1826. Understanding that each of us helps to create history every day, these chronicles project through 2026, when Jackson County will celebrate its bicentennial.

Chapters from our past, present and future are made more vivid through firsthand, personal accounts. "I wish more people had written about (this topic or that) at the time they experienced it," is a common lament among researchers, authors and historians. To try and provide such material, the Jackson County (Missouri) Historical Society collects through donation original, historical documents and photographs and dedicates resources for their long-term preservation so that they may be accessible to future generations.

INTRODUCTION

Acknowledging the wealth of Kansas City–area history that is preserved and made available to the public, I invite you—wherever you are as you read this—to support local history and heritage sites of your choice. Most are owned or operated by nonprofit organizations like the Jackson County Historical Society. Your financial contributions are the lifeblood of such organizations striving to uphold the worthy mission to preserve and promote your history. More information may be found at http://www.jchs.org.

David W. Jackson
Summer 2010
Kansas City, Missouri

BEFORE JACKSON COUNTY (–1826)

A RIVER RUNS BY IT: KANSAS CITY'S ORIGINS CARRIED ON THE MISSOURI RIVER CURRENT

Kansas City is a Missouri River town. That's where this story begins. Before there were towns and cities, streets and highways, there was the river…a broad, winding ribbon past towering bluffs and wooded banks.

The Muddy Mo was a treacherous highway, fraught with snags and subject to floods. But, it was the route of all travel and commerce in those days. It was a course traveled for centuries by Native Americans and newcomers alike. The Missouri River guided travelers as far west as they could go by water passage through the early 1800s to an area that is now Kansas City in Jackson County, Missouri, the "Heart of America."

European American trappers and traders—first Spanish, then French— traveled along the river, learning its secrets from the Osage Indians who called this land home. In 1803, a massive expanse of land that today includes Jackson County became United States territory in the most advantageous real estate transaction in history, the Louisiana Purchase, which the United States purchased from France for roughly one dollar per acre.

The next year, U.S. president Thomas Jefferson enlisted Meriwether Lewis and William Clark to use the river route, a corridor into this vast interior, to mount an expedition to the Pacific. Jefferson's Corps of Discovery traveled up the Missouri River through a continent inhabited by communities of Native American people with traditions and cultures as old as millennia. Before Lewis and Clark reached the Pacific, their

Earliest (circa 1848) view of Kansas City's riverfront (formerly known as the Town of Kansas or Westport Landing) drawn by Hermann J. Meyer. A historical marker erected at the foot of Main Street in June 2010 commemorates this site north of the City Market in downtown. *Courtesy Jackson County (Missouri) Historical Society 005131L.*

exploratory entourage encountered and was assisted by nearly fifty Native American tribes.

The expedition arrived at present-day Kansas City around Independence Day in 1804, where they marked the first Fourth of July west of the Mississippi by firing the keelboat's cannon and naming Independence Creek.

"MAN IS ARRIVING, MAN IS ARRIVING, MAN IS ARRIVING"

Looking on from the riverbank, the Native Americans began a new chapter to their oral tradition, a perspective captured in a libretto created for the bicentennial of the Lewis and Clark expedition. Celebrated classical music artist Rob Kapilow teamed with Blackfeet tribal member and innovative artist Darrell Robes Kipp to create *Summer Sun, Winter*

The Lewis and Clark statue at Clark's Point atop Quality Hill in downtown Kansas City. Also featured in this larger-than-life statue are Sacagawea (Native American guide), York (African American slave) and Seaman (the dog). *Courtesy the author.*

Moon, reflecting the enduring legacy of this historical event. Its second stanza, "Two hundred winters ago a new song was heard in the winter moon's yelling across the rivers. Man is arriving Man is arriving Man is arriving," begins the conversation.

Today, a magnificent, larger-than-life statue overlooks breathtaking vantages at Clark's Point on Quality Hill, located at Eighth and Jefferson in downtown Kansas City.

In September 1808, Clark directed the construction of Fort Clark (later, Fort Osage). Four years previously, in June 1804, he had spotted the prominent point as the perfect location for a federal fortification on the westernmost frontier of the United States. There, a military garrison was established to oversee trade between the Native and European Americans. It was also where the Treaty of Fort Clark (also known as the Treaty with the Osage, or the Osage Treaty) was signed on November 10, 1808 (ratified on April 28, 1810). The Osage Nation ceded all the land east of the fort in Missouri and Arkansas north of the Arkansas River to the United States. Further Osage lands were ceded in a second treaty signed at St. Louis, Missouri, in 1818, and a third signed at Council Grove, Kansas, in 1825.

In her book, *Kansas City Women of Independent Minds*, author and local historic preservationist Jane Fifield Flynn named Berenice (Menard) Chouteau as the "Mother of Kansas City." In 1821, Francois Chouteau, a French fur trader from St. Louis, arrived in the region accompanied by his young wife, Berenice. The Chouteaus eventually built a fur-trading empire along the banks of the river at what is now Kansas City. The Jackson County Historical Society maintains a series of historical markers and offers a self-guided driving tour of Kansas City's French heritage.

In the spirit of Flynn's nomination of Mrs. Chouteau as the "Mother of Kansas City," I appoint Mrs. Mary (Easton) Sibley, wife of Major George Champlin Sibley, the factor or government trade representative at Fort Osage, as the "Mother of Jackson County."

Mary (Easton) Sibley came to this area after her marriage on August 19, 1815, more than a decade before Jackson County was officially organized in 1826. The Sibleys left St. Louis on October 1 and took a thirty-day keelboat entourage up the Missouri River from St. Louis to Fort Clark as it was then known. The fifteen-year-old bride wrote home to her father: "We could only go about four or five miles a day because of the current. The banks of the Missouri are covered with timber. Occasionally an Indian would shoot an arrow from behind a tree, but never hit us. We never saw a white settler from the time we left until we got within a mile of the fort."

In 1819, the first steamboat reached what would become Kansas City. Traffic on the great, muddy highway was about to explode. In 1821, when

Le Soldat du Chene (or Voithe Chinga), second chief of the Little Osage nation and one of the principal chiefs who witnessed the signing of the treaty at Fort Osage on November 8, 1808. *Courtesy Jackson County Historical Society 003738L.*

the state of Missouri was admitted to the Union, William Becknell made a daring decision to save himself from debtor's prison by embarking on a trading expedition to the Spanish territorial capital of Santa Fe in Mexico. Becknell's route was originally called the Mexican Road, which became the Santa Fe Trail, an international trading thoroughfare that would endure for years to come.

Fort Osage remained a part of the fur-trading system until the U.S. government ended the factory system in 1822; but it remained a military storage facility in support of Fort Atkinson, Nebraska, until 1827, when both were closed and Fort Leavenworth was established.

After Fort Osage was decommissioned, the Sibleys returned east and founded Lindenwood College, the first female college west of the Mississippi River.

Fort Osage is an impressive day trip, and it is a real gem that Jackson Countians boast. The fort and adjacent educational center are real charmers, and they provide an intimate view of life and early Native and European Americans in Jackson County more than two hundred years ago.

The meandering drive to Sibley, Missouri, is enchanting. After parking, your first educational experience grows before you. Wildflowers, grasses and sedges native to Missouri have recently replaced modern turf. The diversity of flora is much like that to which the early explorers, pioneers, traders and trappers were accustomed. This natural laboratory provides habitat and food for birds, bees and all kinds of Mother Nature's critters. And, as we come to better understand our place in an ecosystem and responsibility for protecting nature, this new element at Fort Osage is quite timely.

Sibley Cemetery originally served as the burial place for those garrisoned here and the families that settled around the ancient fort.

A twenty-first-century, LEED-certified education center, complete with a "green roof," offers a gift shop, temporary exhibits and first-class permanent exhibits on the geology, flora, fauna and life and times of the Osage Indians, and their interactions with the early traders and trappers.

Fort Osage's reconstruction started with archaeological excavations beginning in 1941 (there have been a total of six archeological digs through 2006). President Harry S Truman congratulated responsible parties through telegram at the dedication of the first blockhouse in 1948: "You are helping all Americans to a fuller understanding of our great past and are advancing the valuable and important movement to conserve those places which remind us of it."

In November 1961, Fort Osage was Jackson County's first site to be listed as a national historic landmark. It is also a national archaeological district, with four known archaeological sites in Fort Osage Park. In the 1980s, Jackson County Parks and Recreation, owners and custodians of Fort Osage, moved from static exhibits to a living history approach that engages visitors much more fully.

Much of this history, briefly outlined here, transpired in only a quarter of a decade. Imagine the many people who experienced these first twenty-five years of "settlement" in the "wilderness."

The next fifty-year period of these chronicles starts with the organization of Jackson County in 1826 and extends to 1876.

FIRST FIFTY FOUNDATIONAL YEARS (1826–1876)

NATURAL MINERAL SPRINGS ONCE POURED LOCAL FLAVOR

Just over fifty years after the signing of the Declaration of Independence, the Missouri General Assembly organized Jackson County on December 15, 1826. At that time, Independence as the county seat was nothing more than a small clearing in the trees near a popular spring.

Tourists looking to beat the summer's heat often ask a thirst-quenching question: "Why wasn't Independence settled closer to the Missouri River?" One simple answer is that settlers needed fresh water and wood for subsistence and, in the early 1820s, found those resources bountiful about three miles south of the precipice of the river's cliffs. That may also be why John Calvin McCoy platted, on the western border of the United States, Westport about as far from the Missouri River in 1838.

Early Jackson County pioneers were drawn to the nineteen or twenty natural springs that were available on the high ground that became Independence. While most watering holes ended up on private land, some remained available to the public. Others drew attention at the turn of the twentieth century for their flavorful and medicinal properties.

The popularity of the J.B. Forbis spring, named after an 1868 immigrant to Independence, "flowed" back to a time when it was used by Native Americans, French trappers, traders watering their livestock while following

Here's Your Old Friend
Polly'
WITH HIS NEW
Carry Home
Carton
6 GIANT 12-ounce BOTTLES 25^c
"AMERICA'S BEST BEVERAGE BUY"

Advertisement for Polly's Pop in the *Independence Examiner* newspaper on April 1, 1949. The company was situated at and used fresh spring water from the Forbis Spring in Independence, Missouri. *Courtesy Jackson County Historical Society.*

the Santa Fe Trail and later by farmers herding their livestock to the Kansas City stockyards. It even became a noontime resort of boys attending the adjacent Ott School before Henry Kloos, a homeopathic physician, acquired the land, covered the spring and converted it into bottling White Springs Mineral Water. Eventually Louis L. and Dorothea Compton used the spring's water in their Polly's Pop soda distribution. Today, while the water no longer runs freely to the surface, the Forbis spring is part of the Independence City–owned Polly's Pop Green Space.

Another such spring flowed at the former Harvey Vaile estate (today the Vaile Victorian Mansion, 1500 North Liberty Street, Independence, Missouri). Miss Carey May Carroll, under her subscription company, Vaile Pure Water Company, bottled its water and sold five-gallon jugs of "pure lithia water, with lithium salts." It was a big attraction to the summer hotel developed as the Vaile Inn.

J.D. Cusenbary migrated to Jackson County about 1840 and had a 322-acre farm between Independence and what would become Kansas City. After an industrious life in a variety of pursuits, Cusenbary, in 1900, proposed a racetrack on his farm. The attraction grew and expanded to become the wildly popular Fairmount Park. Then there was his mineral spring, which had long been known. Publicized for its medicinal properties, it was described in detail, including a chemical analysis, in the 1881 *History of Jackson County, Missouri*. The spring eventually fed into what became Fairmount Park's lake.

The National Frontier Trails Museum in Independence comprises the site of the former Waggoner-Gates Milling Company, descendant of a gristmilling industry that had been on the site for many years. The spring that fed onto the property was long regarded as a watering hole for countless migrants passing through Independence on westward trails. The springhead and its meandering ravine were filled in with the rubble from a 1967 explosion and destruction of most of the complex where Queen of the Pantry flour was produced. Perhaps, one day, this important spring will be excavated and brought back to life. A statue at the Museum of the Pioneer Woman waits with her water pail in hand.

All of the old springs in the 240 acres that became Independence are now "dry," including the four spring-fed wells at each corner of the historic Independence Courthouse Square. One exception is the trickle of the restored Big Spring at the corner of Noland and Truman Roads, part of the Pioneer Spring Cabin interpretive site, which is open to the public.

THE ABUSE AND ACQUITTAL OF REBECCA HAWKINS

Laura Thatcher Ulrich said, "Well-behaved women rarely make history." This insight holds true to the real-life story of one experienced Jackson County pioneer, Rebecca Hawkins, who made history in the 1830s when, in desperation, she took the law into her own hands.

Rebecca, an illiterate mother of five and pregnant with her sixth child, had no choice but to follow her husband, Williamson Hawkins, when he picked up and moved his family west from their Tennessee home in 1830. They traveled by wagon and settled in newly created Jackson County, where Hawkins began accumulating land. Within eight years, he retained 1,680 acres of land, two gristmills and ten slaves. The chain of events that follows took place along the Little Blue River where in 2010 stands the Eastland Shopping Center at the confluence of M-291 and Interstate 70 Highways.

Rebecca bore three more children, and the family appeared to be living solid, hardy, pioneer lives. But under the surface lurked a dirty secret. For nearly twenty years—all her married life—Rebecca Hawkins suffered the physical abuses inflicted by her husband. She was a battered homemaker. It was common knowledge in the small, rural Jackson County community that her husband, under the influence of whiskey, routinely beat and whipped Rebecca, as proved through historical documents presented by biographer William B. Bundschu in his book, *Abuse and Murder on the Frontier: The Trials and Travels of Rebecca Hawkins: 1800–1860*.

In 1838, Rebecca sought a home remedy to her desperate situation. She stirred white arsenic ratsbane poison into her husband's coffee. Her initial attempt to end the attacks by removing the attacker failed (and there's evidence she may have tried poisoning him *twice*). Still, Williamson, ill from the effects of an unknown plague, made out a lengthy last will and testament.

Meanwhile, Rebecca resorted to Plan B. She paid $150 to her next-door neighbor, Henry Garster, to administer another form of poison—a lethal dose of lead poisoning by way of a gun. Rebecca assisted Garster by removing a portion of the mud chinking between the logs of her house by the side of the chimney through which Garster took aim with a squirrel rifle and shot Williamson in the heart while he was sitting asleep before the fireplace.

Unfortunately for Garster, he was tracked to his house by footprints he left in a light layer of snow and ultimately paid for his part with his life in the first *legal* hanging in Jackson County in 1839. Rebecca was arrested at the time of Williamson's burial and later tried and acquitted on charges of aiding the murder. But she was convicted on charges of poisoning based on testimony quoting a conversation with her own slave, Mary.

Bundschu writes:

> Rebecca…could well have been a model for the statues of "Pioneer Mothers" placed along the [trails…as she] certainly endured the variety

Abuse and Murder on the Frontier cover artwork by Ernst Ulmer, showing Henry Garster aiming to shoot Williamson Hawkins through the chinking on his log cabin. *Courtesy William B. Bundschu.*

of hardships and loneliness that the sculptors and sponsors of the statues had in mind. They might not have endorsed her final remedy for one of the all-too-frequent hardships—spousal abuse—but they would have understood the pain that drove her to use it.

What was the fate of Rebecca Hawkins? Her life's story is presented in *Abuse and Murder on the Frontier* (available from the Jackson County Historical Society) in short, easy-to-read chapters and packed with detail that all add up to answering the complex question as to whether her experience was typical or unique among women on the Missouri frontier. It also yields interesting information about various aspects of everyday life in Jackson County in the 1830s.

Log Courthouse Served as the First Seat of Justice

Much has been written over the years about Jackson County's past. Stories are passed on, some growing to tall tales. For reliability, investigation into original, primary documents provides confirmation. This process also sometimes gleans "new" discoveries that might have been overlooked previously.

A vast collection of such documents is being prepared for public access that will offer a wealth of firsthand local stories for researchers to explore. Hidden in these files are long-lost and forgotten stories of daily life, as told through our ancestors' litigious pasts. Here's one fascinating true story to whet your appetite:

Jackson County's "founding fathers" of the county court (analogous to today's county legislature) first convened in 1827 to begin the process of setting up civil government. At that time, Independence Courthouse Square was a mere clearing in the woods. Bids were requested for construction of a temporary log courthouse. The court appropriated $175 but accepted the low bid of $150 from Daniel Lewis. Construction of the two-room log house featuring two rock chimneys and a puncheon floor—logs with one side hewn smooth—appears to have been completed by 1828. The logs of this first courthouse were hewn from trees that stood on the same site where the cabin was then constructed. Sam Shepherd, an African American slave, is credited among the expert adz men. At the time of its construction at the southeast

Sam Shepherd, according to the 1860 census, was born in Virginia in 1810. He came to Independence in 1824 and helped to construct the first log Jackson County Courthouse in 1827 as a seventeen-year-old African American slave of James Shepherd. During the Civil War, he went to Lawrence, Kansas, and remained there until he died. This image purportedly was taken when he was 102. *Courtesy Jackson County Historical Society 000672L.*

corner of Lexington Avenue and Lynn Street (a parking lot as of 2010), it was the last county courthouse between Independence and the Pacific Ocean.

An early grand jury was drawn. It consisted of twenty-four men and adjourned after one day's session. In July 1827, the court reconvened for three days, and the grand jury returned its first indictment against William Reed for horse stealing. He was acquitted for lack of prosecution.

In November the same year, a circuit court convened. It lasted two days, after which the indictment was returned against the first woman ever tried in Jackson County, Missouri. Hannah, an African American slave, was convicted of assault with intent to kill. For a reason that has not yet been recovered, Hannah had tried to kill another slave in a "free-for-all" fight that took place in the slave quarters. The fact that both parties were slaves probably had much to do with the trial and the adjustment of the punishment. Were the crime committed at that time against a Caucasian, there was only one adjudication—hanging without the formality of law or an inquiry into details. True to the customs of those days was Hannah's punishment. It was the decree of the court that she be stripped and given thirty-nine lashes on her bare back, "well laid on," and committed to the custody of Jackson County sheriff Joe Reddeford Walker until the costs of her case were settled. She was allowed to work for the sheriff in payment of the costs, amounting to about five dollars. But who was her master? What became of Hannah? Did she live long enough to enjoy freedom after Emancipation? If so, what surname did she assume? Did she have children? Questions requiring additional research—the answers may never be found.

Serving as a courthouse until 1836, when a permanent brick courthouse was erected in the middle of Independence Square, the "temporary" log structure served many other uses through the years, including a store and a private home. In 1916, it was donated to the City of Independence by Christian Ott Jr. and then moved to its current location at 107 West Kansas in Independence. In the 1920s and 1930s, it housed the headquarters of the Community Welfare League, with Bess Truman serving as honorary vice-chair. Today in 2010, the 1827 Log Jackson County Courthouse is available for tours.

HISTORIC RED BRIDGE CROSSED THE BIG BLUE RIVER

Doubtless few of the commuters who daily cross the Red Bridge over the Big Blue River (just west of Blue River Road) know the significance of the area they are driving through.

The Red Bridge area has existed as an attractive and stable residential area for nearly half a century. But the area's recorded history transports back some two hundred years when explorers like Daniel Boone visited the area, and mountain men like Jim Bridger actually settled; he owned a large farm across from Watts Mill along Indian Creek where Interstate 435 is in 2010.

Early settlers and transient travelers along the Santa Fe Trail also mingled with Native Americans at a trading post along this stretch of the famous route. Visit Minor Park's picnic area located immediately west of the bridge on the south side of Red Bridge Boulevard. As you stand in this vicinity of the bridge, look southwest and picture in your mind processions of Conestoga wagons heavily loaded with goods being pulled by oxen as they were led back and forth between here and Santa Fe (then in Mexico) from 1821 to the

1840s. Rare remnants of the actual Santa Fe Trail survive today as swales, or grass-covered wagon ruts. And you are standing right in their path. About halfway up the hillside, you might spot the large commemorative marker that stands in the middle of this ancient trail.

Wagons had to take their chances fording the often unruly waters of the Big Blue River long before bridgework. Settlers homesteading farms in this picturesque countryside as far west as New Santa Fe (visit the interpretive Trailside Center, 9901 Holmes Road, Kansas City, Missouri), then at the edge of the United States, necessitated a safer river crossing.

Colonel George N. Todd, a fifty-year-old Scottish stonemason, built the first red bridge in 1859. The span at the Old Blue Ford, located one-quarter mile north of the present-day bridge, was one hundred feet in length. Like a picture from *The Bridges of Madison County*, the original wooden bridge rested on stone piers and featured red-painted shingling on its roof and sides, originating a namesake for the bridge, road and surrounding area.

Westward view of Red Bridge Road on its approach to the Red Bridge, circa 1932. The stone pillars are the gates to the home of Bryce Smith, former mayor of Kansas City. Photo by Dick Millard for *Results of County Planning. Courtesy Jackson County Historical Society 009328X.*

A steel and timber bridge, also painted red, replaced the original bridge thirty-three years later in 1892, at the location of the current bridge. George W. Kemper, a Hickman Mills carpenter, removed the original bridge. Some of the timber was recycled into a barn on Solomon Young's farm; other timbers were taken to the John Henry Kemper farm.

In 1932, Solomon Young's grandson, Harry S Truman, as presiding judge of the Jackson County Court (akin to today's Jackson County Legislature), oversaw the design, bid and construction of the steel, concrete and red granite Red Bridge that motorists used eighty years later.

Winding Red Bridge Road may have been a favorite of Truman's because of the bridge's connection to his grandfather; it is the most thoroughly and beautifully photographed area of any other that appears in a book Truman helped the Jackson County Court produce in 1933 called *Results of County Planning*. This volume documented the numerous successes Jackson County had achieved as a result of long-range, strategic planning with regard to infrastructure and protection of natural and historic resources at the beginning of the Great Depression.

The tradition and scenic beauty of the established neighborhoods along Red Bridge Boulevard are evolving today in 2010 with road improvements and a new red bridge that will span not only the Big Blue River but also the railroad tracks running through this "little piece of country in the city." The 1933 bridge will be maintained as part of a walking and biking path. With such a historic area significant to the American West, it is hoped that the visual palette will retain the scale, aesthetic and historical integrity of historic Red Bridge.

REDISCOVERY OF THE RICE FAMILY PLANTATION CEMETERY IN RAYTOWN

The small, ancient cemetery of one of Jackson County's earliest families was rediscovered by two families in the Kansas City suburb of Raytown, Missouri. It was an especially exciting find because the graves are some of the earliest recorded extant burials in Jackson County. And the Archibald Rice family's plantation home has been nicely preserved as a historic site for the public to enjoy as the Rice-Tremonti Home at Sixty-sixth Street and Blue Ridge Boulevard in Raytown.

The impressive marble tombstone of Sally Rice, wife of Archibald Rice, uncovered in the backyard of one Raytown home, revealing the Rice Plantation Cemetery. *Courtesy the author.*

The Morgan family's dog unearthed a peculiar stone one crisp autumn day. It turned out to be the tall, thick, ornately carved marble headstone for the wife of Archibald Rice, Sally (1794–1852). The next-door neighbors reported distinct depressions on their side of their adjoining fence line; likely slave burials.

Archibald Rice, a cotton planter, his wife, Sarah "Sally," their six children and African American slaves settled south of Independence in Jackson County, Missouri, in 1833. They had emigrated from Caswell County, North Carolina, to Monroe County, Missouri, in 1826. The family moved west to the present-day Raytown area around 1837, and by 1844, the cotton-turned-corn planter had built a large home in a semicircle of slave cabins on seven hundred acres. (About five contiguous acres survive today.)

Archibald died in 1849. The next year, Sally was in the 1850 U.S. Census with her son, Coffee, age twenty-six; and daughter Minerva, age twenty-one. Sally then owned sixteen slaves, who were listed solely by age and gender.

When Sally died, most all of her property, slaves included, went to her son, who was likely already living at the Rice plantation with his wife, Kitty, and

An 1840s log cabin of Sophia White (aka Aunt Sophie) on the Archibald Rice Plantation at Sixty-seventh and Blue Ridge Boulevard in Raytown, Missouri, as it appeared in 1957. *Courtesy Jackson County Historical Society 006266L.*

her slave, Sophia "Aunt Sophie" White. Their 1860 census report included thirteen slaves; one thirty-six-year-old female was likely Sophia. The historic log structure known as Aunt Sophie's cabin might be more recognizable to passersby than the Rice home. The cabin has weathered many years and has a fascinating story in itself, not only because it has lasted all these years and for what the cabin represents but also because of one of its former occupants.

Aunt Sophie's cabin was the last of several such cabins to remain after a widened Blue Ridge Boulevard was built in 1914. Sophia lived and worked from the cabin, originally consisting of three rooms, that overlooked the wagon road serving as the Santa Fe Trail (and later the Oregon–California Trails). Sophia fled with her owners to Texas after Order No. 11 instituting martial law was issued during the Civil War. Remarkably, the Rice plantation home and Sophia's cabin were untouched during the mass destruction that occurred when the order was enforced. Even after emancipation, Sophia stayed on with the Rice family, who returned to Jackson County after the war.

Sophia White never married. She remarked once that she had never had time. She claimed she was a fifteen-year-old slave when she became the personal nurse to her master's daughter, Catherine "Kitty" Stoner White, who was born August 11, 1832. That would make Sophia's birth about 1817. Then, when Kitty married E.C. Rice on November 11, 1850, Sophia (then about thirty-three years old) was given to Kitty as a "wedding present." Stories have survived that tell of Sophia visiting with people in her later years about all that she had seen pass by her way as Raytown grew from a small village. She cooked the meals for the household over her own cabin fireplace and carried the food into the "big house." According to Ethylene Ballard Thurston, Sophia scorned the modern cookstove inside the family's house.

For part pay, Sophia was given young livestock that she tended and sold. She was also allowed to peel, dry and sell all the apples she wished from the large orchards on the property. She apparently loaned money to Mr. C (that's Coffee Rice) each year for the interest he paid her. Her savings had grown to $750 when she died around the age of seventy-nine on March 29, 1896; she left it to her mistress's daughter, Anne (Rice) Lane Dunn.

Coffee (or Elihu Coffee Rice) is buried in Woodlawn Cemetery in Independence with his wife, Catherine "Kitty," and Sophia "Aunt Sophie" White.

The last known record of the Rice Cemetery was in 1934 when the Kansas City Chapter, Daughters of the American Revolution, prepared a tombstone inscription index of the cemetery's then existing nine stones. The families are dedicated to doing the right thing, and the Morgans are respectfully planning a private memorial garden over the location of the cemetery that remains in the corner of their backyard.

Should the Friends of Rice-Tremonti Home create a mock cemetery on their property, it would be advisable for them to have the ancient tombstones replicated for outdoor display so that the originals may be preserved and avoid future deterioration and vandalism.

CALIFORNIA GOLD RUSH: A LOCAL NUGGET OF AMERICAN HISTORY

Gold was discovered at John Sutter's mill in the California Territory on January 24, 1848—nine days before the Mexican War ended with the signing of the Treaty of Guadalupe Hidalgo. Sutter, by the way, had previously been a mercantilist in Westport (present-day Kansas City, Missouri).

News spread like wildfire, and people from all corners of the world began to catch the California fever. Countless Americans were on the verge of rushing from the confines of their burgeoning country to the distant western territory. Whether embarking by land or sea, they would set their sights on the California mining country in hopes of realizing their dreams of "striking it rich quick." They would become known as the forty-niners.

By 1850, the number of people moving to California greatly exceeded those headed for Oregon. Two brothers who were ancestors of mine, James and David Lee Campbell, of Clayton, Adams County, Illinois, "caught the gold fever," too. The Campbells recorded their experiences not only in a daily diary but also in a series of fifty-plus letters written home to their families between 1849 and 1852.

The Campbells spent six months in the spring and summer of 1850 walking beside a covered wagon from Illinois through Missouri, "jumping off" at St. Joseph, to California. They arrived on the Pacific coast on September 9, the day before California was admitted to the Union as the thirty-first state. "The boys are going to mining," David Lee wrote to his parents that day. Their immediate discovery was *not* gold, however. They found overcrowded mines and little chances of success, especially with the influx of prospectors arriving daily.

With the majority of the migrants heading for the mines, it did not take the boys long to realize they would yield a far more dependable "fortune" farming in the San Jose Valley.

David Lee and Martha (Fruit) Campbell. *Courtesy the author.*

31

Left: James and Elizabeth (Bradney) Campbell. *Courtesy the author.*

Below: The 1836 Jackson County Courthouse on Independence Courthouse Square, the rendezvous, outfitting and jumping off point for westward travelers between the 1820s and 1860s. *Courtesy Jackson County Historical Society 004862L.*

For the next year and a half, the Campbell boys worked with their uncles at farming and operating mercantile stores in San Jose and San Francisco.

Their uncles, Charles, William and Thomas Campbell, had crossed the plains from Independence, Jackson County, Missouri, in April 1846. They started from Independence Courthouse Square in the large wagon train of more than 250 wagons that included the ill-fated Donner Party. Along the journey the Donners and others decided to take a newly discovered route to California, which left them stranded in the snow of the Sierra Nevada Mountains. Forty-eight people survived the ordeal; another forty-one victims perished.

The Campbells' 1846 wagon train reached California safely and just in time for them to participate in the last months of the Mexican War.

James and David Lee Campbell sailed home from San Francisco on April 17, 1852, and crossed the Isthmus of Panama, which was accomplished by mule, boat and railroad, to the port of Navy Bay on the Caribbean Sea. Setting sail again, they stayed overnight in Havana, "on the hand of Cuba," before arriving in New York. On their migration west toward Illinois, James and David Lee Campbell saw Niagara Falls before returning to the young brides they had left behind a year and a half before.

Today we are still fascinated by the gold rush decade and the ordinary people who lived through one of the most extraordinary events in the history of the United States. The Campbells were ordinary people who did the extraordinary thing—they recorded their experiences. Descendants saved and graciously donated the historical documents to the American public for posterity. Enjoy their story and discover if they struck it rich in *Direct Your Letters to San Jose: The California Gold Rush Letters of James and David Lee Campbell, 1849–1852* (Kansas City, MO: the Orderly Pack Rat, 2000), available at http://www.orderlypackrat.com. The National Frontier Trails Museum and the Oregon–California Trails Association, both in Independence, are invaluable resources, too.

Gilliss House Hotel Registered the Far Western Frontier

Gilliss House Hotel stood on the Missouri River at the fledgling Town of Kansas in the mid- to late 1830s. It was a structure known to every traveler to the west in those days.

Kansas City lost the famous Gilliss House Hotel long ago, but its foundations are recoverable in the Missouri Riverfront "Town of Kansas" archaeological park, slated as one of Kansas City's future redevelopment attractions.

Another relevant artifact harkens to the Gilliss House Hotel's past—a guest book that dates from Tuesday, September 7, 1869, through February 4, 1870, preserved at the Kansas City Museum.

Known at various times as the Claiborne House, the Western, the American, the Eldridge and the Union Hotel, Gilliss House Hotel stood majestically beside the Missouri River at Westport Landing since the origin of the Town of Kansas and through the infancy of Kansas City.

William Gilliss, who for a number of years was its landlord, constructed the Gilliss House Hotel or hostelry in 1846–47 as a two-story brick building of very modest dimensions. The fame of the cuisine and the good cheer of the bar traveled far up and down the river.

Gilliss was assisted at times in the early days of his hotel career by his future brother-in-law, Dr. Benoist Troost. After striking it rich in the California gold rush, Troost returned about 1852 and married Gilliss's sister. Gilliss House Hotel quickly showed the effect of Troost's newly acquired wealth after the two became partners.

One of the most exciting and thrilling episodes of the Border War occurred at the Gilliss House Hotel when Kansas governor Andrew Reeder, fleeing east for his safety, hid there for twenty-four hours from his hot-blooded enemies, who were clamoring for his life. Reeder narrowly escaped in a creative disguise with the help of the proprietors.

By 1860, Gilliss House Hotel was again undergoing renovations that included beautiful carpets and wallpapers and new elegant furniture for the ease and comfort of guests of the Gilliss House Hotel who were passing through on their westward journey.

This fascinating guest register was first discovered in 1891 by Fred Hacker, a plumber, who was doing some repair work and found it in a deserted closet of the old hostelry. The register was carelessly placed in Hacker's shop at 400 Delaware (in the City Market), where it became buried beneath a clutter of pipe fittings and tools. He even took the liberty of using the register as his own personal scrapbook by pasting cancelled checks on a few pages.

In 1912, one of Hacker's workers uncovered the guest book once again. It was donated to the Missouri Valley Historical Society, and after that organization ceased operations, the book was donated to the Kansas City

Gilliss House Hotel on the Missouri riverfront greeted riverboat passengers when the Town of Kansas was the last stop on the western frontier. *Courtesy Jackson County Historical Society 004439L.*

Museum at Corinthian Hall (3218 Gladstone Boulevard, Kansas City, Missouri) between 1940 and 1942.

The oversized ledger contains autographs of hotel guests from near and far. While some signatures were penned in florid, Spencerian script, others were less elegant. One famous guest was George Armstrong Custer. Just imagine the conversations as guests signed in!

On the day this book was first opened, sixty-four guests registered; the following day, thirty-four signed in. Some guests had their own rooms—up to four guests shared the same room on these first two days. With more time and attention to additional names, it is quite likely that this guest book will yield more fascinating details. It makes me wonder: does Holiday Inn keep registers of its guests today for posterity?

POOR FARM IS A MAJOR MEDICAL CENTER TODAY

Jackson Countians should recognize their longtime commitment to caring for underprivileged citizens.

In the early days the Jackson County Court (forerunner to today's county legislature) "boarded-out" by allotting funds for private parties within the community to provide room and board for those who could no longer care for themselves.

Figuring that it would be more efficient to administer one institution rather than doling resources to individual caretakers, the county court purchased for $1,000 a 160-acre parcel of land from Henry Washington Younger (father of the infamous Cole Younger) in rural Jackson County. This became Jackson County's Poor Farm (which technically was an almshouse, or poorhouse, with a large working farm connected to its operations). The site was on high ground in the Blue Hills countryside overlooking the scenic valley of the Little Blue River. Eventually, the property expanded to more than 300 acres with several institutional buildings. The first appointments for a superintendent and physician were filled by March 1852.

By July 1908, the cornerstone of a new building changed the name of the institution to the Jackson County Home. This building became—and is still in operation today—as a long-term care facility for indigent elderly. By the 1930s, the institution was referred to as the Jackson County Home for the Aged and sometimes the Jackson County Home for the Aged and Infirm. In the days of segregation, a separate "nursing home" was located across the street for African Americans.

In 1928, Harry S Truman, as presiding judge of the Jackson County Court, campaigned for and saw passage of a bond issue leading to the construction of the three north-facing wings that were added beside the Jackson County Home. The east and west wings were three stories high and the center was four stories (the fourth floor was constructed for hospital purposes; a mid-1970s addition connected the two buildings). A few years later, as thirty-third president of the United States, Truman's interest in a national health insurance program anchored him as one of the first national leaders to make healthcare funding a priority.

In the midst of the Great Depression, the Rural Jackson County Emergency Hospital in 1937 provided twenty-four-hour emergency services. Like the Jackson County Home for elderly residents, the hospital's twenty-one medical and surgical beds and four maternity beds were occupied by county residents who were without funds and by emergency cases from automobile accidents on rural highways.

The Jackson County Hospital as it appeared, circa 1933. Formerly the Jackson County Poor Farm, the functions of that 1852 institution continue today at the Truman Medical Center. Photo by Dick Millard for *Results of County Planning. Courtesy Jackson County Historical Society 009398X.*

The facility, faculty and patient care have evolved into today's Truman Medical Center at Lakewood, a state-of-the-art healthcare facility at the former site of Jackson County's Poor Farm. Reminders of the farm are the historic structures that have been preserved and integrated into the modern facility. An in-depth study of this history is available in the *Jackson County Historical Society JOURNAL.*

FRONTIER JUSTICE AND THE 1859 JACKSON COUNTY JAIL

In 2009, the oldest structure on the historic Independence Square turned 150—the 1859 Jackson County Jail and Marshal's Home.

A souvenir book published by the Jackson County (Missouri) Historical Society, *LOCK DOWN: Outlaws, Lawmen and Frontier Justice in Jackson County, Missouri,* documents the origin and evolution of the structure. Captured here are excerpts offering skeleton keys to unlocking history of the early lockdowns, of those who defied frontier justice and the systems and strongmen (and their overlooked wives) who tried to keep law and order in Jackson County, Missouri.

On November 4, 1858, the Jackson County Court ordered the clerk to solicit designs for a jail. At the February 1859 term, the plans of prominent pioneer Kansas City architect Asa Beebe Cross were adopted. The 1859 Jackson County Jail is the earliest documented surviving structure designed by Cross.

In 1859, the former brick Jackson County Jailhouse that had been built next door in 1841 was sold to Major Granville D. Page, who traded African American slaves at the site. Construction of a new Jackson County Jail and jailor's residence—using slave labor—was completed in March 1860. The site survives and, since 1959, has been owned and operated by the Jackson County (Missouri) Historical Society as the 1859 Jail, Marshal's Home and Museum.

But you cannot now, nor could you then, see the imposing jail from the street. The two-story, twelve-cell, limestone jail adjoins the rear of the brick home that fronts Main Street. Each cell's window was fitted with heavy iron, stationary louvers that, while allowing minimal sunshine and fresh air, provided little protection from the elements. In 1907, a new, two-story brick

The 1859 Jackson County Jail as it appeared in the 1877 *Illustrated Historical Atlas of Jackson County, Missouri* (reprinted in 2007 by the Jackson County Historical Society). Since 1959, it has been owned and operated by the society as the 1859 Jail, Marshal's Home and Museum at 217 North Main Street in Independence, Missouri.

structure with numerous iron cells was added. After being decommissioned by Jackson County government in 1933, iron cells were removed to transform the area into project workspace, primarily for Works Progress Administration (WPA) activities.

A recent document uncovered during research for *LOCK DOWN* was an 1871 Missouri statute making Jackson County unique in Missouri, with the establishment of the office of marshal of Jackson County, an elected post that was to be filled *in addition to* the traditional sheriff of Jackson County.

When the marshal's position was abolished fifty-three years later in 1924, a longtime employee at the courthouse, Dell Womack, said, "As I recollect the chief reason Jackson County was given a marshal was [the sole purpose of catching] Jesse James."

LOCK DOWN also provides details about legal hangings, notorious outlaws and all the Jackson County officials between 1826 and 1933, including an extensive biography of the first county marshal—Major Granville D. Page, (mentioned earlier)—whose Missouri River Gothic home a few blocks west of Independence Courthouse Square survives as a private Independence residence today in 2010.

Prior to 1871 when the marshal's position was created, the principal occupant of the Jackson County Jail was likely the jailor. Perhaps the most noted jailor—at least the most well-documented one—was Henry Bugler, who was assassinated on June 13, 1866, while in charge of his duty as jailer (his six-year-old son was also wounded by a stray bullet). Bugler's pregnant wife, Mary, was kept on in charge of the jail (*and* her six young children) for some time after her husband was killed. Pinch your copy of *LOCK DOWN* today at http://www.jchs.org!

PICNICKING UNDER THE LONE JACK TREE

Commemorating the gallant Civil War heroes—North and South—who fell at the August 16, 1862 Battle of Lone Jack became the biggest thing in the southeastern part of Jackson County for years. The idea of having a picnic and reunion originated on August 16, 1870, when the monument to the Confederate dead was dedicated (the earliest *Kansas City Star* record found was in 1885).

Sally (Cave) Grinter remembered attending many such events and recorded and deposited her recollections with the Jackson County Historical Society. Her family belonged to the Lone Jack community "and we children looked forward to the 16th of August as we looked forward to Christmas. We began thinking and planning for it days ahead. It was spoken of as 'the 16th,' 'are you going to the 16th?' or 'I'll see you at the 16th.'"

People came from near and far, some camping on the grounds. "Once we were frightened nearly to death when a band of gypsies passed by. Hadn't we heard wild stories about them carrying off little girls?" remembered Grinter. Relatives and friends who had left the community planned to return for a visit at that time of year. As the day approached, folks consulted their farmer's almanacs and prayed for a clear, sunny day.

Grinter said:

> *On the morning of the 16th, everyone was up early. At the barn the horses were curried until their coats shone in the sun, and the spring wagon that had been washed and polished the day before was rolled out. There was a new whip in the socket and Major, the family dog, who knew there was something on foot, frisked around in ecstasy. I dreaded to see the hurt in his eyes when he was told to stay at home.*

As they neared the shady, grassy, sixty- to eighty-acre grove of walnut and elm trees of the picnic grounds two miles southwest of the Town of Lone Jack, there was a man on a horse with a big red sash across his shoulder who directed traffic. The picnic grounds were called Griffith's, Overton's or Russell Brothers' Grove, depending on the owner of the property at any given time; once, in 1906, the picnic was located one mile east of town at Shawhan's Grove. Band music could be heard playing, the tunes growing louder as the throngs drew nearer.

The picnic was not a lunch or dinner but a banquet. At noon, large white linen tablecloths were spread on the grass, for there were no tables on the picnic grounds. People sat on the grass or stood while eating.

> *Home cured ham…was the queen of the feast. It had hung from the rafters in the closed smoke house over a smoldering fire of hickory chips until it was saturated with smoke and cured for keeping. After being slowly baked*

The former Civil War battlefield became the site of the annual Lone Jack picnic, which eventually included a stump for those seeking political office. *Courtesy Jackson County Historical Society 006059XX.*

in the oven of a wood stove, trimmed and dotted with little black cloves, it was superb.

Great platters of brown, crusty fried chicken fried in half butter and half-sweet, country-rendered lard were followed by meat courses and many bowls of salad: potato, cabbage slaw, corn salad, beets and a raft of pickles—sweet and sour, mixed and whole.

Then came desserts. The women of the community had enlisted their heirloom recipes from their grandmothers in North Carolina, Kentucky or Tennessee to bake pies and cakes: white cakes, yellow cakes, dark cakes, pound cakes, ribbon cakes, marble cakes, hickory nut, hazelnut, raisin—all iced to perfection from these gifted mothers' hands.

Drinks included cold water from nearby springs that was dipped into barrels and placed at different places over the grounds. Coffee and other drinks were brought with the food.

As if to tempt one still further, at last there were huge watermelons that had cooled for days in the outdoor caves and spring-fed wells.

The picnics were great friendly get-togethers of the people. In Mrs. Grinter's humble opinion, "they vied with the churches in being the means of healing wounds in the hearts of the people caused by [the Civil] War… The old men sat around in groups; many of them were in their soldier uniforms. Those wearing the blue and gray were friends again and argued good naturedly about the War."

"Finally in the late afternoon," Grinter concluded, "father began to round up the children, and after many 'good byes' and 'God bless yous' they started for home."

In later years, the picnic became the pulpit for local politicians.

The Battle of Lone Jack Museum was dedicated on August 16, 1963, and is a site worthy of support and recognition.

WHEN MARTIAL LAW REIGNED IN JACKSON COUNTY

Six years before the outbreak of the Civil War, terrorism reigned in and around Kansas City. Kansans favoring abolition migrating primarily from northern states came into conflict with Missourians, where three-fourths of the 1860 population was sympathetic to southern traditions reliant upon slavery. Widespread bloodshed, daily skirmishes and clashes between neighbors typified escalating guerilla tactics.

In 1861, Colonel Jennison, of the First Kansas Cavalry, issued an edict to Missourians along the border counties that their property would be confiscated, houses burned and nobody would be spared who refused the proclamation. William Clarke Quantrill responded in January 1862 by organizing the first band of about twenty Confederate Missourians. These irregular, or guerilla, forces grew in numbers, attacked and surprised their enemies by stealth and fought to protect themselves and their property.

Quantrill's posse was ambushed and narrowly escaped a blazing house fire at New Santa Fe (at about 125th and Wornall today). Osceola, Missouri, was set afire. In retaliation, there was a "massacre" at Centralia, Kansas. The Union prison collapse in downtown Kansas City, Missouri, killing and injuring southern women, is said to have caused Quantrill to raid Lawrence, Kansas.

Mrs. Mattie Lykins (later Mrs. George Caleb Bingham) was there. Her original recollection was donated by a descendant, Mr. Robert Dewitt Owen, in memory of his grandmother, Mrs. Dewit Livingston (Ada Campbell) Owen, to the Jackson County Historical Society:

> *I was an eye witness to the Lawrence Massacre and the rigid enforcement of Order #11...It so happened the morning Quantrell [sic] entered Lawrence that I got up to lower the window shades in my room, just as the morning sun was beginning to redden the eastern horizon. A view of the entire town with the beautiful prairie surrounding it lay before me like a lovely picture. All was quiet and peaceful as though the roar of the cannon had never been heard in our land. I had scarcely laid down again, when I heard rapid firing. My bed stood near a window from which a good view of the town and prairie could be had. Leaning over the foot of my bed I drew the curtain aside and looked out in the direction of the firing. I saw a number of horsemen riding to and fro and could plainly see the smoke from their guns. Without the slightest suspicion of what was transpiring I sat up in bed and watched them until the firing ceased. After which they fell into line four abreast and rode rapidly down Massachusetts St., to the Eldridge House where they halted. In a few moments, a white sheet floated from one of the windows which I took to be the work of a chambermaid cleaning up rooms, but it proved to be a flag of truce unfurled by the Provo Marshall of the State who chanced to be in the hotel. In an instant after this, the horsemen spread over the town in every direction*

W.J. Courtney, who was with Company B, Shank's Regiment, Fifth Missouri Cavalry, Shelby's Brigade, Price's Army, provided his impressions of the events that led up to Ewing's "infamous, devilish order":

> *The capture, sacking, and burning of Lawrence, Kans., after that was in retaliation for the sacking and burning of Osceola by Jim Lane and his men more than a year before. The fight and massacre, as it has been called, at Centralia was in retaliation for the killing of one of Anderson's sisters and the crippling for life of another by undermining and throwing down a house in Kansas City in which they, with other Southern women, were confined.*
>
> *Missouri was isolated and cut off from the Confederacy. There was a Federal garrison in most every town in the State. A manifestation of sympathy for the South meant banishment, confiscation, and destruction of property or death. There was no law. The courts were terrorized,*

and officers were military puppets of the power. Fire and sword reigned supreme, and the guerrillas and bushwhackers simply paid back the insults and wrongs to which they and their families and their friends were subject. They fought in the only way in which they could fight, and they fought to kill. William Anderson was killed in a fight with Curtis's command at Orrick, Ray County, Mo., in the fall of 1864, and his body was dragged through the streets of Richmond, Mo., by the Federals. Quantrell [sic.] survived the war and died in Kentucky some time later.

Trying to control vigilante justice, Union general Ewing issued General Orders No. 11 (commonly known as "Order No. 11") a few days later in August 1863, requiring all Southern sympathizers to vacate their homes and remove from Jackson County, under pain of death.

Brutally enforcing the order, some Union forces abused their power. Eyewitness accounts document the cruelty of homes and crops being burned; destruction of livestock; people being killed without cause or proof of crime; and possessions being looted. Missouri artist George Caleb Bingham was the only Union soldier to protest publicly. Refusing to plunder and kill, he later painted *Order No. 11* or *Martial Law* depicting these atrocities. Bingham married the widow Mrs. Lykins in 1878, at about the time Bingham was distributing copies of *Martial Law* as an engraving. The Jackson County Historical Society's engraving, signed by Bingham, has been reproduced and is available for sale.

In Jackson County, family lore accompanies a Bible that survived Order No. 11. When Mrs. Cyntha Hudspeth's home was maliciously burned and the embers were still red hot, she instructed one of her slaves, Sam, to rake through the ashes and salvage any possessions that might have survived. Sam's obituary more than forty years later confirmed the family tradition:

Sam Jackson was owned by the Hamiltons and the Hudspeths of Fort Osage Township…[He] was fond of telling stories of the times before the war, and one was of a miracle he saw with his own eyes. The old log house known as the Hudspeth home in Fort Osage Township was burned by the Federals under the famous Order No. 11. Mrs. Hudspeth was a very old and devout lady and she had the record of her family in an old family Bible which, at the time of the fire, was in a cupboard in the old house. When the house was smoldering the old lady called

George Caleb Bingham's *Martial Law*, or *Order No. 11*, which was first exhibited at Polk, Dyer & Sharp's Auction House, 823 Main Street, on New Year's Eve and New Year's Day 1868. The proceeds for the benefit went to the Widows' and Orphans Home (which was the institution founded by Bingham's wife, Mattie (Livingston) Lykins Bingham). Photograph by Kansas City photographer W.T. Dole. *Courtesy Jackson County Historical Society 004009L.*

to Sam and pointed to a place where the fire had been the hottest and ordered him to take a long handled rake and dig into the coals. She told him he would find her Bible there unharmed. [He] dug into the coals and got out the Bible, which was scorched around the edges of the heavy leather cover, but unharmed inside. Old Sam always referred to this as a miracle.

This Bible is now in the collections of the Jackson County Historical Society because of the foresight of a descendant, Mrs. Dora Slaughter, of Buckner, Missouri. Readers interested in donating original documents and artifacts relating to Quantrill, Order No. 11 or the Civil War in Jackson County are invited to contact the historical society. There they will continue to be preserved and made useful to the public into the future.

ALEXANDER MAJORS'S DRAMATIC LIFE AS AN OVERLAND COMMISSIONER

While the Pony Express did not run through Jackson County, one of its founders lived in our area. The Alexander Majors palatial home—according to 1850s standards—is preserved for visitors at Eighty-second and State Line, a small corner that once comprised extensive acreage.

Majors amassed and lost several fortunes in his lifetime. Among other ventures, he also had a large tract of property north of Lone Jack.

The Russell, Majors and Waddell Pony Express venture was his most notable but short-lived (eighteen-month) achievement.

Majors, a religious man, apparently had a penchant for adventure with nomadic inclinations. Born in Kentucky in 1814, his father moved the family to Missouri four years later. They crossed the Mississippi River at St. Louis on a flatboat propelled by three Frenchmen. The ferryboat was only large enough to carry one wagon at a time, without the team. Majors married Katherine Stalcup in Jackson County on November 6, 1834.

The forty-five-year-old "overland commissioner" and family were enumerated in the 1860 census in Nebraska City, Nebraska (their real estate was valued at $22,500 and personal property a staggering $791,150). I wonder if *that* home survives…and how it compares to the one they left behind in Jackson County during the Border and Civil War period. Majors's business ventures went bust in the 1860s; his marriage crumbled; and he left everything and everyone behind.

Mr. and Mrs. Majors were plagued in their later years with poverty. His wife and one daughter were even admitted to Jackson County's Poor Farm under assumed names to avoid ridicule from friends and neighbors. They claimed at the time that Alexander had abandoned them, leaving them destitute.

By 1870, Majors lived in a boardinghouse in Corinne, Utah, dealing in lumber. Within ten years, in 1880, he was still alone but operating as a "mining broker" in Helena, Montana.

Just over a decade later, around 1892, William F. "Buffalo Bill" Cody found his former boss in Denver, Colorado. (You can find a portrait of Majors in the Denver State Capitol Rotunda.) Majors—who had given Cody his first job as a boy, had taught him to read and write and employed him as a freighter—was without money and had hardly enough to eat. He was trying to write the story of his life on the frontier, but his manuscript was all over

Alexander Majors's home and descendants. Original identified by Louisa Poteet Johnston, a great-granddaughter of Alexander Majors. For more information, the 1880 U.S. Census enumerates all of these people together. *Courtesy Jackson County Historical Society 000435L.*

the floor of his cabin when Cody visited. They struck a bargain: Majors was to finish his book; in return, Cody paid all his expenses until it was ready. He paid the cabin rent in advance and guaranteed it indefinitely, and he instructed a grocer to give Majors unlimited credit.

When Cody returned after a year in Europe with his Wild West Show, Majors had written enough for several books. In the end, it was edited by Colonel Prentiss Ingraham, trimmed, and published by Rand McNally & Company in Chicago, Illinois. Although *Seventy Years on the Frontier* never made Majors a fortune, it continues to be reprinted over and again after more than a hundred years.

Cody sent Majors to take charge of his Scout's Rest Ranch in North Platte, Nebraska. That didn't last too long because, in January 1900, Majors died at age eighty-six in Chicago. He was laid to rest in Union Cemetery with little ceremony at the funeral.

KANSAS CITY'S HANNIBAL BRIDGE LAID RAILS TO FUTURE

Imagine the days when wagon trails were giving way to the speed and predictability of railroad rails. The July 1869 Independence Day celebrations in Kansas City were frenzied when the grand opening and ribbon cutting of the very first railroad bridge to cross the Missouri River was completed at Kansas City, Missouri. It was actually a phenomenal day for U.S. and engineering history, too.

Recognizing the 140th anniversary of this monumental event, the Jackson County (Missouri) Historical Society "poured some coal" on a project to reprint the original copy of the book published by the bridge's chief and assistant engineers, Octave Chanute and George Morison. *The Kansas City Bridge: With an Account of the Regimen of the Missouri River and a Description of the Methods Used for Founding in that River* was published in 1870.

Chanute was born in Paris, France. He immigrated to the United States with his family at age twelve. The 1850 U.S. Census shows Chanute staying at the Marshall Tavern in Hyde Park, New York.

He held a number of professional positions over the next seventeen years prior to moving to Kansas City to build the Kansas City Bridge for the Hannibal and St. Joseph Railroad. He became a naturalized U.S. citizen and married Annie Riddell James of Peoria, Illinois (with whom he had six children).

According to local historian and Chanute aficionado Bill Nicks, Chanute's 1867 move to Kansas City was to bridge the "rapid, shifting, and ill-reputed" Missouri River. At the time, many thought it was impossible to bridge the mighty river due to the swift and dangerous currents. Chanute managed to subdue the river as a testament to his own expertise, the advice and experience of the local Native American Indians, early settlers and bridge-builders on the Rhine River in Germany.

The bridge connected seven railroads and made Kansas City the dominant city in the Missouri valley, edging out the then much larger cities of Leavenworth, Kansas, and St. Joseph, Missouri, which also had wanted the bridge. At the time, *Harper's Weekly* identified Kansas City as a town "not so well known in the East as Leavenworth, Omaha, St. Joseph." Chanute's assistant on the bridge construction was George S. Morison, who thirty years later became instrumental in building the Panama Canal.

View of the Hannibal Railroad Bridge, looking to the northwest from the hill at the foot of Walnut Street. Photo from the James Anderson photograph album. *Courtesy Jackson County Historical Society 000696L.*

Nick's research reveals that Chanute also built the Union Stockyards in Kansas City. During the summer of 1869, being a bit of a land speculator, he platted and subdivided the towns of Lenexa and Columbia (later renamed Hillsdale), Kansas.

In 1889, Chanute began corresponding with many contacts across the globe who were interested in conquering the air. Through his writings and his experiments, Chanute established himself as an expert in aviation. On May 30, 1899, Wilbur Wright wrote to the Smithsonian Institution seeking advice on mechanical human flight. The reply contained a list of publications on aerial navigation. Included on the list was Chanute's book, *Progress in Flying Machines*. A year later—May 13, 1900—Wilbur Wright wrote to Chanute the first of what was to become nearly five hundred pieces of correspondence between Chanute and the Wrights.

FIFTY GOLDEN YEARS OF EXPANSION (1876–1926)

FOLLY THEATER'S MAJESTIC STANDARD

A story into history awaits you at every street corner. Take the corner of Broadway and Central in downtown Kansas City where the Grand Old Lady of Twelfth Street has stood the test of time. In 1900, renowned local architect Louis Curtiss designed the vaudeville house we know today as the Folly Theater.

When it was constructed as the Standard Theater, audiences cheered chorus lines of dancing girls, acrobatics, comedy, jugglers, songs and comedic acts grouped under the guise of vaudeville. They also marveled at the sheer magnificence of the structure that boasted, among other ostentations, electric light bulbs—an invention introduced in Kansas City only a year earlier.

Appropriately, the Standard's name changed in 1901 to the Century Theater, where it welcomed "legitimate theater" with the world's top entertainers. Near the end of the first quarter of the century, however, vaudeville and burlesque returned during a roaring time when hemlines rose, the *Titanic* sank and America tried dry-docking during Prohibition.

Even though talkies (or motion pictures) and girlie shows increased in popularity, for nearly a decade between 1923 and 1932 the theater legitimized itself again with national players like the Marx Brothers, Humphrey Bogart and Shirley Booth under the ownership of a

The Standard Theater (today the Folly Theater). *Courtesy Jackson County Historical Society 000956L.*

prominent New York–based family who renamed the venue Shubert's Missouri Theater.

The Great Depression and World War II tremendously affected American society and cultural landscapes. Of all Kansas City nineteenth-century theaters, for instance, only the Missouri ended up surviving the wrecking ball; its name changed for the third and final time to the Folly Theater in the 1940s. The forms of entertainment also devolved over the years from lighthearted burlesque to striptease and even to adult films in the late 1960s (giving a whole new meaning to the phrase "if these walls could talk").

By the early 1970s, foresighted Kansas Citians began a quest to "strip the Folly." You would never guess from looking at "her" today, but it took seven years of diligent, dedicated, hard work (starting with the cleanup of 9.5 tons of pigeon droppings in the attic) and millions raised in funds to restore and "redress" the beauty on Twelfth Street to her original grandeur.

Today in 2010, we enjoy a diverse offering of entertainment at the Folly Theater, which celebrated in 2000 her first century. If Kansas Citians are to continue to boast and brag about this community cornerstone through to the end of this century, they each need to make a commitment to support the fine work of those who keep the Folly's doors open.

Take a virtual historical tour at http://www.follytheater.com and keep abreast of future "Folly Flashback" slide presentations offered occasionally by the Folly Theater.

VOLKER'S LEGACY OUTLIVED ANONYMITY

This is another true, unique Kansas City story with a lesson for each of us. It's about how one humble citizen gave back to his community during his lifetime, and how sixty years after his death, Kansas Citians continue to benefit from his selfless generosity.

Relocating with his extended family from Chicago to Kansas City, he expanded his home furnishings and window shade business to include offices in a dozen cities.

In 1890, he purchased a new three-story, twelve-room, brick-and-shingle Kansas City Shirtwaist house at 3717 Bell Street. His two-acre wooded lot was where his mother raised a vegetable garden and kept a cow and chickens and his father grew flowers and a variety of roses, for which the estate eventually was named Roselawn.

Then, in 1911, the fifty-two-year-old bachelor married, bequeathed $1 million to his bride and set out over the next thirty-six years to give—that is, invest—more than $10 million in local philanthropic causes. Though revered by the time he died on November 4, 1947, he preferred anonymity. In fact, he gave away an estimated one-third of his wealth, much of it secretly, for which the *Kansas City Star* dubbed him "Mr. Anonymous of Bell Street."

This German native gave generously to an endless number of charities, including: the Helping Hand Institute (today the Helping Hand of Goodwill Industries, which has preserved its early photographs in the Jackson County (Missouri) Historical Society's archives); the old German Hospital (today Research Hospital); and the University of Kansas City, including hundreds of thousands of dollars for residences, buildings and property known today as the Volker Campus of UMKC.

William Volker's
Roselawn.
Courtesy the author.

There was assistance for the Jefferson Home for Women and Children, the Florence Home for Negro Girls, the Andrew Drumm Institute for Boys, Children's Mercy Hospital and Wheatley Provident Hospital (the only private hospital in Kansas City for African Americans).

He started a retirement fund for schoolteachers, established a profit-sharing plan for his employees, purchased animals for the Kansas City Zoo and gave not only to his own church but to others as well.

His countless gifts to individuals were wide ranging and generally helped people help themselves through employment or educational pursuits. Biographer Herbert C. Cornuelle, in his book *Mr. Anonymous*, described an endless stream of people—in good times and bad—approaching him in his office for a dime or a dollar, which he freely gave.

William Volker's Helping Hand Institute in the City Market of downtown Kansas City has been converted to lofts. *Courtesy the author.*

Beyond the financial assistance he broadcast, his example of modest, gracious living is worth emulating. This unassuming Kansas City couple lived in the same home in which they had started housekeeping. And their beloved estate is still intact today, much as their family left it. Take a drive after shopping and dining along the Thirty-ninth Street corridor some day, and enjoy the peaceful Kansas City neighborhood anchored by Roselawn.

Hopefully, the home, outbuildings, gardens and champion trees that compose Roselawn—a Historic Kansas City Landmark—may remain intact for future Kansas Citians to appreciate…and to be reminded of the power of one individual to make the world a better place. Such is the legacy of Mr. William Volker.

CORRALLING JACKSON COUNTY'S PRIZED STOCKYARD BUSINESS

In light of today's terrorist, biological and environmental threats, imagine how the hostilities of the American Civil War paralyzed most day-to-day operations across our country, and decimated communities and industries, without discrimination.

Union and Confederate soldiers surviving the horrors of the battlefield had to subsist between skirmishes. Often fending for themselves, they confiscated foodstuffs and livestock. A scarcity of commodities after the war included beef. But sizeable herds of Texas longhorn cattle grazed in the Southwest.

Getting cattle to hungry eastern markets saw the advent of cattle drives and the American cowboy, who herded longhorns out of New Mexico and Texas and up through Oklahoma to the nearest railhead at Abilene, Kansas. Cattle buyers would then load their commodities on train cars headed east toward Kansas City.

But getting goods, including beef, from Kansas City to eastern markets was an obstacle because of the wide and muddy Missouri River. Providentially, foresighted Kansas City promoters and politicians managed to get the first railroad bridge across the Missouri at Kansas City. The Hannibal Bridge was dedicated in 1869, and Kansas City steamed forward full throttle to become the second-largest rail center in the country, second to Chicago. The railroad bridge, and the "stampeding" cattle industry, helped transform the small Town of Kansas into metropolitan Kansas City.

As cattle from the Southwest were shipped from Abilene into Kansas City, they were transferred to other rails heading out in every direction to eastern markets. The holding pens constructed to transfer cattle became the famed Kansas City Stockyards, Jackson County's first million-dollar industry. After the advent of refrigeration, packinghouses could provide "prepared" meat to market.

Having overcome transportation challenges, producing better quality beef became a priority for the industry. One inferior trait of Texas longhorn cattle was that their slender hindquarters made tough meat, particularly cuts of steak. Jackson County farmers responded to the demand for better steak by trying to breed a better bull. To protect money generated by the new cattle industry, bankers and corporate leaders began establishing vast farm

Kansas City Stockyards in the West Bottoms, circa 1890s. *Courtesy Jackson County Historical Society 011509X.*

estates across eastern and southern Jackson County in an attempt to be the first to develop a new breed of beef cattle.

Suddenly, livestock breeding became fashionable, and each ranch or estate competed to outdo the other. Cattle were imported from Europe and the United Kingdom and crossbred as breeders searched for perfection. Jackson County became the Cattle Capital of the country.

Simpson and Gudgell, an Independence outfit, finally made the right connection with a bull obtained in England named Anxiety IV. Much of the beef available today is American Polled Hereford, the product of the perfect beef first sired by Simpson and Gudgell on their ranch along Noland Road, south of Twenty-third Street.

It's hard to imagine in today's sprawling Kansas City metropolitan area that cattle and agriculture were once vital to Jackson County. What happened to those huge livestock, dairy and produce farms, some of which were still in place in the mid-1960s? Little primary documentation has yet been donated. The Jackson County Historical Society welcomes additions of written historical information and original photographs that "corral" for future citizens this area's rich livestock lineage and agricultural heritage.

BUCOLIC BIG BLUE RIVER VALLEY'S PAST AND FUTURE

This is a "swell" story, one that will "ripple" in your mind for some time to come. Pick up an oar and paddle with us as we explore the origin and evolution—and contemplate the future—of Jackson County's Big Blue River Valley.

The Big Blue River is fifty miles long; ten streams are its tributaries. Its headwaters are in Johnson County, Kansas, south of Olathe. It flows across the Kansas-Missouri state line on its way through Swope Park, meandering toward and eventually emptying into the Missouri River at Big Blue Bend.

One branch of the trails that headed west through Jackson County from the 1820s to the 1860s followed Independence-Westport Road and crossed the Big Blue River at about present-day Twenty-eighth Street to Twenty-eighth Terrace.

In the Civil War days, the Battle of the Big Blue occurred on the riverbanks of this winding, aquatic highway. Old-timers relayed that when General Pleasanton chased General Sterling Price from Westport to the Big Blue, Price dumped three brass cannons into the Big Blue River.

Eastern manufacturers and local real estate agents created a boom for Kansas City in the middle 1870s, and the Big Blue River Valley became a main attraction. Motorists commuting today via Interstate 435 between the Missouri River and Eastwood Trafficway will traverse a rather unsightly stretch that formerly were bustling Jackson County "towns" (technically subdivisions) platted between 1887 and 1890. Each town was built around a factory either established or at least financed with English capital, thus their predominantly English names: Manchester, Centropolis (north of Manchester) and Sheffield on the west bank of the river; Leeds; and Pittsburg on the west, opposite of Manchester. (The town of Birmingham was also platted on the north bank of the Missouri River in Clay County.)

Each of the towns in the valley had a mushroom-like growth with frenzied financial ventures. Then a serious depression, the nationwide Panic of 1893, forced the demise of nearly all businesses in the entire valley. In 1897, after the worst of the panic was over and new industries began to come into the Big Blue River Valley, the Kansas City city limits were extended. On April 6, 1909, another extension was made and included

Canoes and houseboats on the Big Blue River, circa 1900. *Courtesy Jackson County Historical Society 000881BL.*

that part of the valley south of Eighteenth Street and east of Topping and Hardesty Avenues.

Over the next thirty-five years, numerous business concerns located in the Big Blue River Valley. The oldest and longest lived was the Kansas City Nut and Bolt Company, which later became Sheffield Steel, then Armco.

Near the turn of the twentieth century, as recreation and leisure for the working class were "invented," a plethora of small excursion boats began to appear on the Big Blue River. The Kansas City Boating Club was born, as was the Missouri Canoe Club, Kansas City Yacht Club, Paddle and Camp Club, Star Canoe Club, Women's Boat Club and Blue River Yacht Club.

George E. Kessler, landscape architect who planned the park and boulevard system of Kansas City, together with the Kansas City Board of Parks and Recreation commissioners, had long planned for the beautification of the Big Blue River, preserving its banks for pleasure purposes, with a ten-mile-long parkway meandering from the Missouri River to Swope Park.

However, the natural beauty was lost to industrial expansion—work that would continue to change the valley for the next forty-plus years.

The Works Progress Administration (WPA) continued city-sponsored work of changing, straightening, widening and deepening the channel to try and prevent flooding and control storm water runoff—work that would carry on through the 1980s.

Given its appearance today in 2010, it's hard to believe that Daniel Morgan Boone (third son of the famous Daniel Boone of Kentucky) was among the first European American traders and trappers of this area. He made the journey alone in 1787 at age eighteen from Kentucky through the trackless wilderness to the little trading post called St. Louis, where he spent a dozen summers. His winters were spent trapping along the Little and Big Blue Rivers. Boone described in his memoirs the winters he spent camping and trapping on the Big Blue River and said this region was the best beaver country he knew. As best as can be pinpointed, Boone's camp on the river was a little south of the Twenty-seventh Street Bridge on the west bank, where there is a rock ledge outcropping.

Is our very own paradise lost? Will we ever be able to restore beauty and aesthetic to the Big Blue River Valley? Is a parkway or extensive green space out of reach? These are just some questions to ask yourself as you drive along the Big Blue River on Interstate 435 or on the Truman Road Bridge over the rock and concrete viaduct of the Big Blue River.

THE ENDURING CHARM OF SWOPE PARK'S LAKE OF THE WOODS

It's one of my favorite places in Kansas City, perhaps because it is connected with my earliest and most fond childhood memories. It may also be somewhat of a secret to those unfamiliar with Swope Park beyond the developed landmarks (namely the Kansas City Zoo and Starlight Theater) near the park's formal entrance off Meyer Boulevard and Swope Parkway.

I'm referring to the Lake of the Woods, which—as it turns out—is a man-made lake created more than one hundred years ago.

A horseshoe-shaped lagoon was excavated early in spring 1908, and the reservoir that was to supply it was formed by building a huge dam thirty-five feet high and nearly one hundred feet long across a small branch through which the waters of the Big Blue River escaped into a natural basin. The area of the water surface of the Lake of the Woods is ten acres. The lagoon, which is six feet lower than the lake, is twenty-five and a half acres (it measures exactly a mile in length around its outer bank).

Fifty Golden Years of Expansion (1876–1926)

Thus was the "confluence" of the Lake of the Woods. A 1908 *Kansas City Times* article reported:

> *It lies in a hollow encircled by a chain of low hills a quarter of a mile south of the park suspension bridge over the Blue. The sides of the hills are covered by a dense growth of trees that extend to the water's edge. In the summer, their overhanging branches will form shady retreats for exploring canoeists to penetrate. A row around the lagoon, which is three-quarters of a mile in extent, through the canal and to the extreme southeastern part of the winding lake will provide an afternoon's exercise for the stoutest paddler.*

The suspension bridge is the famous "swinging bridge" that, like the lagoon, is now incorporated as part of the experience of the zoo's African exhibit.

By mid-December 1908, a "park driveway" (later named Gregory Boulevard) was being graded and prepared for surfacing that would

Lake of the Woods, circa 1920s. Photo by Dick Millard. *Courtesy Jackson County Historical Society 011151BL.*

skirt the west bank of the canal and cross the dam to connect with the county road south of the park (termed Hickman Mills Pike, which became Oldham Road).

Lots of changes have taken place at this location in the last decade. Most notably, Oldham Road—which once meandered north from Lake of the Woods past the lagoon, swimming pool, picnic areas and ball fields northward to Sixty-third Street—was closed at Lake of the Woods when the zoo expanded. The former stone Lakeside Nature Center and Park Ranger post (where patrol officers mounted on horseback were stationed) are currently leased, but adaptive reuse ideas are always being sought.

On several occasions my grandma, Pat Campbell, bagged homemade popcorn (in the days before microwaves made popcorn easy) into empty plastic Wonder Bread sacks. After my half day of kindergarten at Blue Ridge Elementary in Raytown, the school bus dropped me off at my grandparents' house, and Grandma and I would often drive to the Lake of the Woods. We would feed a flock of fidgety white ducks where a new shelter house was recently constructed. The ducks were so rambunctious that this five-year-old would have to stand on the concrete picnic tables to keep from getting pecked. When our bread bags of popcorn were empty, it was home to watch cartoons like *Wonder Dog*, then a "cat nap" (as Grandma called it) before supper.

THE DAY THE HORSELESS CARRIAGE ROLLED INTO KANSAS CITY

On the precipice of historic alternative energy sources, I'm holding out for an economical plug-in hybrid-electric (PHEV) flex-fuel option that gets more than one hundred miles per gallon (see Google's project at http://www.RechargeIT.org).

This exciting opportunity puts me in mind of the very first automobile to drive on Kansas City streets—an Edison machine using storage battery electricity that would run thirty miles before needing to be recharged—in 1899!

The *Kansas City Star* reported on November 13, 1899, that "The Automobile is Here." A separate, lengthier article that day described fire department chief Hale's investigation into acquiring the first automobile fire wagon ever made in the United States from Chicago's Fire Extinguisher Company.

Jessie A. and Mary Virginia Lyle and Warren E. Brandenburg. The men founded the prolific Photographic and View Company in Kansas City in 1895. Mrs. Lyle married Brandenburg after Mr. Lyle's death. This is Lyle's home at 3834 Forest Avenue. *Courtesy Jackson County Historical Society 006393L.*

The next day, a short news item declared, "Kansas City is so accustomed to up-to-date things that the horseless delivery wagon which appeared on the streets yesterday created no surprise and attracted little attention."

Within a week, the situation was markedly different! The one and only automobile in use in Kansas City, driven by A.D. Boyer, an electrician with the West Bottom meatpackers Swift & Company, "filled every requirement," reported the *Star*:

> *An automobile has been in operation on the streets of Kansas City for a week and is apparently a success. It has not balked at steep hills, run away, backed over the curbing, nor has it caused the horses attached to other vehicles to shy. On the contrary, the horseless wagon which the Swift Packing Company has in use in this city for the purpose of advertising, taking orders and making small deliveries, behaves in a manner becoming*

Richard "Dick" Burke and Pearl Hoskins's filling station and grocery store on the northeast corner of Forest and 24 Highway. *From the Hoskins Service Station Album; gift of Ms. Diane Marshall. Courtesy Jackson County Historical Society 017395.*

a well directed conveyance. Rolling along silently and dodging street cars, wagons, and pedestrians, it attracts as much attention today as it did a week ago when it made its first appearance.

The machine is operated by a single lever that regulates the power from the storage battery, applies and releases the brake, and directs the motion forward or backward. It does not require full power to run on level streets. When a grade is encountered, additional power is applied and the speed is not diminished. No trouble is experienced in crossing and re-crossing street car tracks.

Noiseless, electric "horseless" cabs had been in use in Chicago and New York earlier in the year, according to syndicated reports. Autos were being used for sport in Paris. And industries as far as Santa Fe were boasting uses for the new contraption.

In May 1899, the Electric Vehicle Transportation Company for Missouri was incorporated as one of seventeen companies incorporated by the Whitney-Elkins-Widener Syndicate to operate automobiles in different states.

First Telephones Rang a Bell

Anywhere you drive today it seems like three out of five motorists have one hand on the wheel with the other holding a tiny cell phone to their ear. (Whatever happened to the ten-and-two safety rule I learned in driver's education?) Younger readers cannot remember a time without the cell phone.

Maybe it's worth pulling the string tight between two empty soup cans again and making a long-distance call to the summer of 1877 when Kansas Citians were first introduced to the telephone.

Lee D. Stanley, an avid electrician and night manager for the Kansas City office of the Western Union Telegraph Company, built Kansas City's first telephone exchange—the first telephone exchange west of the Mississippi.

Colonel I.C. Baker, superintendent of the telegraph company, visited Stanley in Kansas City in 1877 and mentioned that his friend, Mr. George Freeland Durant, had just begun canvassing St. Louis to begin installation of a telephone system. Baker invited Stanley to canvass Kansas City, and he agreed. Baker provided Stanley pamphlets, diagrams and rudimentary sample telephones (no dial; just a mouth- and earpiece and a crank with a bell) and promised to provide the wire, instruments and equipment if Stanley could get twenty subscribers.

Stanley had no challenge installing the exchange and making it work. However, he first had to persuade complacent citizens to overcome their view that the contraption was an extravagance; that a telephone would be useful; and, most importantly, to believe that the "thing would talk."

Stanley's canvass was slow going. His first successful converts were six subscribers working in the grain elevators. He then secured Armour & Company, Jacob Dold and Fowler Brothers packinghouses in the West Bottom.

Soon thereafter, the first telephone exchange was installed in a room eight by ten feet, boarded off in one corner of the Western Union operating room. The first telephone operators were three men (two day and one night shift); women were not in public employment at this early date.

According to a March 24, 1905 edition of the *Blue Springs Herald*, a franchise had just been secured to extend telecommunications to Oak Grove, bringing eastern Jackson County in close connection by wire.

Of course, many readers today will remember a time when you picked up the phone and were connected directly to an operator called "Central,"

Blanche Browing (left) on the switchboard at the *Kansas City Star. Courtesy Jackson County Historical Society 010451L.*

who would answer, "Number, please," and put you through to your desired party. By that time we had dial telephones, telephone numbers, exchanges (remember Harrison 1-1200? Westport 1-9999?) and "party lines"—all of which would warrant a feature article in itself.

Here's a novel idea: pick up the phone today and call the Jackson County (Missouri) Historical Society—preferably not while you are driving—at 816-252-7454 if you'd like to donate Kansas City–area telephone directories for years that they are missing (a list is online at http://www.jchs.org).

THE BIRTH OF THE KANSAS CITY ZOO

Kansas City Zoo (http://www.kansascityzoo.org) turned one hundred years old on December 21, 2009. The first mention of a zoo for Kansas City came at a city council meeting in mid-November 1907, when Gus Pearson and W.V. Lippincott, who were members of the Jackson County Humane Society, called for a zoological society.

Offers of rare animals were previously offered to the city, but there was no authority or financial provision to receive and care for them. A plan was proposed for a zoological society to have charge of the zoo and to appoint a keeper and assistants to be paid by the city. "We propose to ask the city also to set off a part of Swope Park for the zoo and to provide proper fencing and shelter for the animals," said Pearson at that first announcement in the *Kansas City Star*.

By January 1908, it was clear that Kansas City was not going to have any trouble making a start of its zoological garden in Swope Park. Pearson reported having received a letter from A. Goerling, a handler of rare animals in western Australia, who offered through the American consul to contribute as a starter and afterward sell kangaroos and other animals and birds to Kansas City.

Then, by late March 1908, the *Kansas City Star* printed a letter from a man in Silver City, New Mexico, who said, "A party has just brought into town a wildcat, captured in the mountains near here." He offered to forward it by express and offered the enticement that "the cat is about two thirds grown and has a very pretty skin."

Parks department employees got into the spirit. A rainy day in May precluded them from normal work, so they went fox hunting in Swope Park. A den containing three Kentucky red foxes was found, and two were captured. B.A. Chandler, then park superintendent, said, "We also know where there are some young wolves, and we'll get them too."

Finally, on June 22, 1908, sixty acres in the northwestern part of Swope Park were set aside for Kansas City's zoological garden. The next month, plans for the first building, a $15,000 structure of native stone, were announced. The 190-foot by 900-foot animal house was erected near the west entrance to the zoo. Groundbreaking for this historic building—which survives today—took place on November 5, 1908.

Fundraising for the purchase of animals for the Swope Park Zoo was first advertised in September 1908. A "stuffed menagerie street parade" of H. Jarret's personal collection of Australian specimens was exhibited to promote the main event that included two lectures at the old Convention Hall (now the site of Barney Allis Plaza) by G.O. Shields, editor of *Shield's Magazine* and director of the then ten-year-old, 260-acre New York Zoological Gardens.

The zoo building shortly after it was built in 1909. *Courtesy Jackson County Historical Society 011149L.*

Shields, author of many books (some under the pseudonym Coquina), including *The Big Game of North America, Hunting in the Great West* and *Rustling in the Rockies*, said, "You can have no idea of the true value of a zoo until you get one of your own."

To boost funding, the Kansas City Zoological Society contracted in April 1909 for another event in the Convention Hall. This time, the Campbell Brothers Circus featured a menagerie of twenty-four cages and a sideshow.

Appropriations for the zoo didn't come forth without a "roar." Before passing, the measure had to be reintroduced to the council. And over the next few months, as work progressed at Swope Park, entanglements between the city and the zoological society delayed opening day.

Upon completion of that first building, the Swope Park Zoo formally opened to specimen animals on December 21, 1909. Another source mentions that the Lemon Brothers Circus, wintering in Dodson (an area in Kansas City south of Waldo), inspired the zoological society to purchase from them three lions, some monkeys and a bear.

Like a procession of Noah's ark, odd and wonderful creatures from around the world populated the zoo over the next few months. By April 1910, we humans were enjoying the happy hirsute family in the Swope collection.

Within a year a *Star* article reported, "There are about as many different kinds of noises in the zoo out in Swope Park as there are cures for a cold; and all of them going on at the same time."

Independence also had the Horne Zoo that started about 1912. Readers with historical material about the Horne or Kansas City Zoos are encouraged to contact the Jackson County Historical Society.

AN UP-TO-DATE HYPOTHESIS

The catchphrase surrounds those who live in Kansas City, especially these days with the polishing taking place in and around town. The term "Everything's Up-to-Date in Kansas City" comes from Richard Rodgers and Oscar Hammerstein II, who made popular an old, local adage in a song called "Kansas City" for their 1943 musical play and 1955 musical film, *Oklahoma!*

I put my "hands on the plow" and dug deeper to "brand" an up-to-date hypothesis to explain the inspiration behind the playwrights' famous refrain.

When "lassoing" details for the title and lyrics to "Kansas City," it is plausible that either the songwriting duo had some connection to or knowledge about Kansas City in 1906 (the year *Oklahoma!* is staged). At least they "circled the wagons" to try and uncover the Kansas City way of life at the turn of the twentieth century. The so-called newfangled inventions touted in the song had come about from five to twenty years before! So one should not interpret that just because the fiction is set in 1906 that all the facts are going to be by the book.

Still, connections to the burgeoning city and the song ring clear.

The lines "I counted twenty gas buggies goin' by theirsel's" and "'Nen I put my ear to a Bell Telephone and a strange womin started in to talk!" allude to the new, modern inventions of the automobile (or horseless carriage) and telephone, which were *relatively* new to our predecessors. The telephone had debuted in Kansas City in 1877; the automobile in 1899.

"They went an' built a skyscraper seven stories high" has traditionally been attributed to Kansas City's seven-story New England Building (which, by the way, is a near exact—if not mirror—duplicate to the New England Building in Omaha, Nebraska), built in 1890. So the song expressing such excitement over the seven-story "new" New England Building doesn't fit the 1906 storyline of *Oklahoma!*

(Next door to Kansas City's New England Building is the much more famous New York Life building at 20 West Ninth Street, Kansas City's *first* skyscraper. It is ten stories tall and was completed in May 1889; again, several years before Rodgers and Hammerstein's production.)

It is likely that the line "They got a big theayter they call a burleeque" refers to the majestic Folly Theater.

But now to my hypothesis about the origin of the theme within the famed song proclaiming "Everything's Up-to-Date in Kansas City"!

In March 1891, the *Kansas City Star* ran a little snippet, the first of its kind, titled "An Echo Up to Date." From then on, and for many years thereafter, this short "Up to Date" irregular column ran short tidbits, jokes, axioms, quips and humorous witticisms, often abstracted from other national publications.

Some were one-liners, others were up to ten to fifteen lines of text, each with their own headline: "Up to date kiss," "Mr. Hoyt's idea of widowhood up to date," "Two old cronies up to date" and "Moses up to date." Occasionally, they promoted new or popular fashions ("Up to Date Hats and Bonnets") and sometimes a brief etiquette lesson ("Up to Date Wedding Invitations").

After reading a series of these, they put me in mind of the funny segment on *Rowan and Martin's Laugh-In* (the NBC comedy-variety television program than ran from 1968 to 1973), where the regulars took turns bantering fast-paced jokes as they peeked from behind small, opening and closing, psychedelic-colored windows and doors.

So where *might* the mystery *Kansas City Star* columnist have come up with the "Up to date" idea in the first place?

Inspiration may have originated in the Kansas City theater world (which would be ironic that it would be rekindled and reach wide acclaim years later in the lineup of *Oklahoma!*).

Just a few months before the debut of the "Up to Date" column, the Coates Opera House had pulled back its curtains for a touring production called *Faust Up to Date*, an English musical burlesque that parodied Charles Gounod's 1859 opera, *Faust*. A burlesque took a well-known play, story, opera or pantomime and satirized it in an exaggerated style with music. *Faust Up to Date* was one of a series of burlesques on popular plays and operas of the day, including *Carmen Up to Date* (mocking the opera *Carmen*) and *Cinder-Ellen Up to Date* (based on the pantomime *Cinderella*).

THE FIRST "UP TO DATE" ENTRY IN THE *KANSAS CITY STAR*
March 21, 1891
"An Echo Up to Date"
"The prize echo has been discovered by a Southern newspaper in
a Kentucky cave. Shout, 'Hello, Smith!' and it will answer, 'What
Smith do you mean?' fourteen distinct times." From Puck

By the time "Up to Date" in the *Kansas City Star* began running, it is probable that readers understood the satirical connotations. They also enjoyed them, which explains the column's lengthy run in the paper.

I'll leave you with one lingering question: "Is your membership in the Jackson County Historical Society 'Up to Date?'"

PRIESTS OF PALLAS: AN ALLURING FESTIVAL

There was a time when all citizens in and around Kansas City anxiously awaited the autumnal arrival of the Priests of Pallas fête.

Kansas City in the late 1880s was straddling two eras. Though poised on the cusp of the Industrial Revolution, it was still firmly rooted in its agrarian economy. The farming and cattle industries of Jackson County and its neighboring communities remained the region's lifeblood.

Yet Kansas City was coming into its own as a metropolis and an important commercial and social center for a vast region spanning several states. It is against this backdrop that the Priests of Pallas festival was born.

The first Priests of Pallas celebration was in 1887, and each year thereafter for the next quarter century this majestic fall festival was the largest social event of the city. Priests of Pallas mimicked autumnal festivals in other cities across the nation. It was emulated after the Veiled Prophet that originated in St. Louis in 1878 and Mardi Gras, renowned in New Orleans since the 1850s.

The original, weeklong Priests of Pallas events took place after harvest, as farmers and ranchers within a two-hundred-mile radius of Kansas City

Above: Ready for the Priests of Pallas Parade in Kansas City, these four ladies were chosen for their beauty. Julia Wilson Lowe (later Mrs. Sam Pendleton) is seated in the rear, far right of the carriage. *Courtesy Jackson County Historical Society 011759L.*

Left and next two pages: The Jackson County Historical Society welcomes donations of photographs pertaining to Kansas City history. These views are from the resurrected Priests of Pallas masquerade balls from 2005 to 2007. *Courtesy the author.*

converged on the city to market their bounty and celebrate. For the farmers, this autumn trip to Kansas City was the culmination of a year's toil. For local businesses, the influx of visitors meant an annual economic boom. For the city's merchants and residents, it was a time of year that symbolized abundance and prosperity and celebration of a bountiful harvest and a robust market.

Each year, a different theme was chosen, and elaborate parade floats illustrating them were constructed on the flatbed chassis of streetcars and motored through downtown streets on rails. The Fête of the Priests of Pallas theme kicked off the tradition in 1887. Some other themes in the years to follow included: Parade of Nations (1889); American History (1890); Grand and Comic Opera (1895); Story of the Stars (1904); and quite a futuristic theme, A Trip to Mars (1909), which included one float called Wireless Messages.

Beginning in 1896, organizers began producing an artifact souvenir. These items (ranging from postcards to figurines, candlesticks to bud vases) are considered collectible today. For the benefit of future generations, the Jackson County (Missouri) Historical Society is striving to assemble—through generous donations—a complete collection of historical Priests of Pallas artifacts.

If the parades were a draw, the Priests of Pallas masquerade ball eventually became the festival's signature activity.

After nearly a quarter century, the decline and demise of the celebration was hastened by the development of a culture of leisure in the 1920s. Kansas Citians had a variety of entertainment choices, including amusement parks and movie theaters, even the American Royal. Then, too, the exciting, newfangled automobile industry and the birth of the "road trip" rendered the heartland's population ever more mobile, opening up a world of diversions that must have made the notion of a harvest festival seem quaint.

NELLY DON TRIED ONE ON AND TOOK IT
FOR A RIDE

We've tried it on, and it fits like a glove. *Nelly Don: A Stitch in Time*, by Terence Michael O'Malley, is an elegantly assembled textile...err...textual history of Kansas City's premier fashion icon. The ninety-page book is loaded with images that "stitch" together for readers a fascinating "pattern" of the life and times of Mrs. Nell (Quinlan) Donnelly Reed, affectionately known by her fashion label, Nelly Don.

A model for the Donnelly Garment Company, showing off the latest Nelly Don fashions from spring 1936. *Strauss Peyton Photographic Studio Collection. Courtesy Jackson County Historical Society 007593L.*

Would you believe this story begins with a simple, pink gingham frock, or housedress, that a young, "discontent" bride with a "slim purse" (her words) designed in 1916? Imagine the day Nell walked into Peck's Dry Goods department store in downtown Kansas City, presented "colorful little aprons" and immediately secured an initial order of eighteen dozen dresses? Nell had just "threaded" a fashion empire.

Fifty Golden Years of Expansion (1876–1926)

Seamstresses of the Donnelly Garment Company in their first industrial plant in the Coca-Cola Building (the Western Auto Building as of 2010). *Courtesy Jackson County Historical Society 012773L.*

Nell became one of the wealthiest and most celebrated American women in business and philanthropy; her company became the largest of its kind in the world. Throughout, she praised and supported the workers who helped Nelly Don "bolt" into the women's garment industry.

Before the stock market crash in 1929, Donnelly Garment Company employed mostly seasonal workers for summer and winter fashion lines. As the Great Depression descended upon the nation, however, Nell used her patented Handy Dandy apron to keep the factory open year-round, giving employment to many in a time of great need.

The apron was unique in that a tailor never had to remove the garment from the machine to sew the seams. Efficiencies like these and innovations, including pioneering the sectionalized method of garment production, became a hallmark for Donnelly Garment Company.

One million dollars from Handy Dandy's revenues also helped Nell buy her husband's interest in the company in November 1932, when her twenty-five-year, strained marriage to Paul Donnelly ended in divorce.

But wait; there are more yarns to weave. As the Donnellys' marriage waned, Paul drank heavily and was notorious for his extramarital affairs. As for Nell, she became enamored with her dashing neighbor, nearly thirty years her senior, former U.S. senator and Kansas City mayor James A. Reed. The attraction was obviously mutual, as the two conceived a child early in 1931. Nell traveled to Europe—ostensibly to adopt a child—with her "confinement" ending in Chicago in September, when Nell gave birth to David Quinlan Donnelly (whose last name would later become Reed).

We hardly have room here to tell you about his mother's kidnapping and father's heroic rescue, when David was but three months old and under the attendance of a governess. Nell and her chauffeur, George Blair, were abducted one night after work as their automobile approached the driveway to the family home (today, the Toy and Miniature Museum, 5235 Oak Street, Kansas City, Missouri). Reed forcefully took charge in pursuing the kidnappers, even enlisting the help of Kansas City political gangster Johnny Lazia, until the event ended thirty-four harrowing hours later. Nell and Reed were married in December 1933.

A decade later during World War II, Nelly Don reconfigured its fashion dress and coat manufacturing plant into producing action clothes for American service women—and those who replaced men in heavy industries. The Historic Kansas City Garment District Museum threads Kansas City's textile history for visitors.

African American Neighborhood of Steptoe Vanishing

Kansas City's newest fire station in Westport on Forty-third Street faces a pre–Civil War-era enclave called Steptoe, a historically village-like African American community, once segregated. As land uses in this neighborhood continue to evolve, Steptoe as a residential neighborhood is one "step" from extinction, prompting the dire need to study, preserve and commemorate this Kansas City original.

Jackson County slave owners include Westport founder John Calvin McCoy and John B. Wornall, a banker and gentleman farmer, who built the antebellum home operated today as the John Wornall House Museum (6115 Wornall Road). They may have traded slaves at auction in the oldest

A nanny and her charge in 1918. *Courtesy Jackson County Historical Society 002730S.*

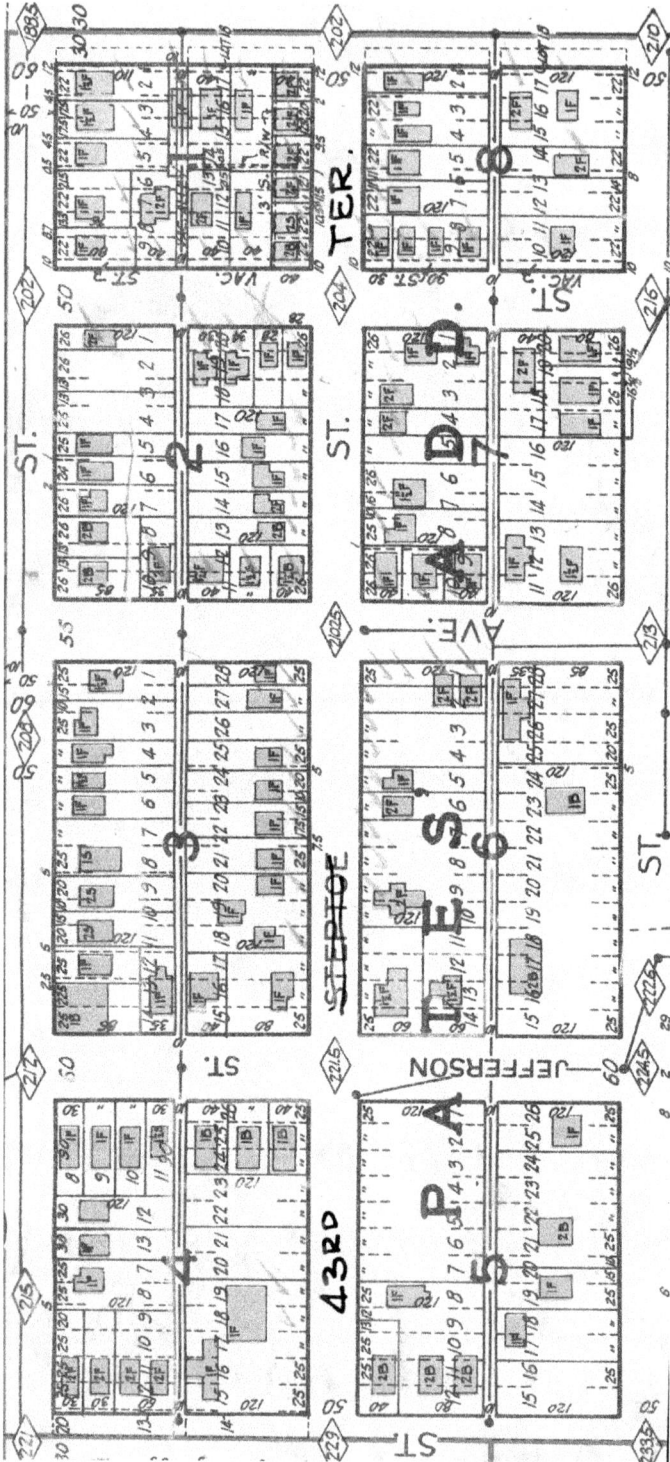

The Steptoe neighborhood from the 1925 *Atlas of Kansas City*. Courtesy *Jackson County Historical Society*.

building in Kansas City, the Albert G. Boone store (today Kelly's Westport Inn) at the northwest corner of Westport Road and Pennsylvania Street. Remarkably though, McCoy established a way for slaves in Westport to become freedmen; that is they could work to buy their freedom. That there was land also set aside for freedmen to own makes this story doubly unique.

According to ongoing research by local historian JoeLouis Mattox, who helped to bring Steptoe's legacy to the forefront, Steptoe's origins date to at least 1857, when Henry Clay Pate, publisher of the *Border Star* newspaper and postmaster of Westport, paid $3,900 for a pasture outside Westport's southern boundary. "Pate's Addition to the Town of Westport" included three east–west streets named Pate, Clay and Steptoe (Forty-third Terrace today in 2010) that were bounded by Broadway on the east and Summit on the west. Like many other Kansas City streets, the name "Steptoe" was once spelled out in blue and white ceramic tiles in the pavement at each corner.

Eventually, the African American population in Pate's Addition grew. Penn School (formerly located at 4237 Pennsylvania), founded in 1868, was the first school west of the Mississippi established for the expressed purpose of educating black children. The St. Luke African Methodist Episcopal (AME) Church was organized in 1879. Another neighborhood church, St. James Baptist Church, located at 508 Pennsylvania, organized around 1883; services are still being held there today.

The tiny, segregated hamlet became a collection of neat clapboard houses tucked along narrow streets. Many residents became chauffeurs, maids or cooks who worked in white neighborhoods surrounding Steptoe, but there were also railroad porters and cooks, plumbers, gardeners and other professionals. Though there were segregationist attitudes, there was little racial tension. Longtime residents called their community "a little island" and talked about having white, Jewish, German, Italian, Hispanic and Swedish people for neighbors, declaring it "the best colored neighborhood in the city."

INDEPENDENCE DAY IN THE HEART OF AMERICA

Have you ever wondered how Kansas Citians celebrated Independence Day one hundred years ago? It wasn't that long ago, really. Here's a blast from our past as you light your sparklers, Roman candles and smoke bombs and as you grill your hot dogs, hamburgers and chicken breasts.

The *Star's* first account of how Kansas City celebrated the nation's birthday appeared in the nearly two-year-old newspaper in 1882 (then known as the *Evening Star*). The *Star's* Independence Day coverage in 1881 had been superseded with news of the assassination attempt on U.S. president James A. Garfield (shot on July 2, he suffered greatly before dying on September 19); naturally, firecrackers were silent in 1881.

First, let's commemorate the earliest local celebration of Independence Day when the Lewis and Clark expedition camped just north of here along the Missouri River in 1804 and "ussered [ushered] in the day by a discharge of one shot from our Bow piece [likely, a swivel cannon]." According to Clark's journal, they also "saluted the departing day with another gun, an extra Gill of whiskey."

With the exception of an issue here or there, newspapers for eastern Jackson County and Independence did not survive prior to 1898. The *Jackson Examiner's* first coverage of the Fourth of July in 1898 reported a successful celebration with a bandstand erected on the Independence Courthouse lawn, speeches, a costumed "Goddess of Liberty," reading of the Declaration of Independence and more. The first *Independence Examiner* newspaper coverage available in 1906 provided an account from "an old soldier," titled "A Submerged War Story," where he relayed the events of the "battle of Gettysburg and siege of Vicksburg culminating on the fourth day of July, 1863." The *Kansas City Star's* earliest coverage of the Fourth was in 1882. Other papers predate this, but that's as far as my fuse has yet burned.

Streamers about July 4 in Kansas City were more elaborate, judging from the 1901 festivities celebrating the quasquicentennial (or 125th anniversary) of the signing of the Declaration of Independence.

Imagine scorching weather in a time long before the invention of air conditioning and when women and men of the Victorian age dressed in smothering layers from neck to wrist to toe—no exceptions.

The mercury broke all records on this day in 1901 since the weather bureau's establishment thirteen years prior. A squelching 103.3 degrees was "recorded by a very conservative government thermometer." In fact, "Kansas and Missouri afforded the highest temperature readings in the country" on July 4, 1901; Harrisonville, Missouri, registered 106 degrees. The highest previous temperature in the bureau's statistics up to that point had been 103 degrees in 1897.

Fifty Golden Years of Expansion (1876–1926)

Fourth of July in Swope Park in 1912. *Courtesy Jackson County Historical Society 002158S.*

Though there was little relief trying to catch a breeze on the streetcars, Kansas Citians enjoyed outdoor public entertainment at local parks, fairs and exposition grounds. Fairmount Park (which was once located along today's Independence Avenue/24 Highway just east of Mount Washington Cemetery between Willow and Harris Avenues) had the largest crowd in its history. The lake was alive with boats, and the beach was thronged. You couldn't get near the big, cool spring. And at the cafés, hotels and counters where refreshments were sold, "one had to wait his turn." All over the expansive lawns tired humanity rested. Parties were too numerous to be accommodated in the picnic grounds, and they were scattered about the entire park.

That night, a magnificent show in the sky was seen through and above the big trees. Band concerts were the most widely enjoyed entertainment for the thousands of people in attendance, and the "arrangement of national airs" was particularly moving. In short, "The Fourth was celebrated noisily, continually and elaborately."

This anniversary celebration was so well attended that there weren't enough streetcars in operation to take everyone home from the park, despite the Metropolitan Railway Company having run all of the cars that its powerhouse could pull on the Independence and Fairmount lines. The last streetcar left Fairmount Park at midnight. Many who missed late-night connections to Kansas City had to walk home.

This 1901 Fourth of July celebration is a snapshot of life before radio, television, movies, TiVo, computers, DVDs, iPods, etc. In fact, electricity was so new that most homes in Kansas City weren't yet wired. The automobile had not yet replaced the horse and wagon.

SOME UNPLEASANT HAPPENINGS ON PLEASANT STREET

A series of tragic events began transpiring in the prominent Swope Mansion in October 1909. Three deaths and several other Swope family members struck with typhoid fever (when there were no other cases in Independence) led some to suspect foul play and a plot to plunder the significant Swope fortune.

The foreboding Swope Mansion on Pleasant Street (where the Campus RV Park is situated in 2010; the mansion was razed in the mid-1960s) was the setting. *Unpleasant* were the details presented in the first book to chronicle this mysterious chapter in Kansas City history, *Deaths on Pleasant Street: The Ghastly Enigma of Colonel Swope and Doctor Hyde*. Giles Fowler's fascinating story is prime fodder for a leading Hollywood mystery movie.

What followed was a nationally publicized trial akin to the O.J. Simpson trial of 1994–95, except there ended up being three trials. Law students to this day often study the Swope Murder Trials. The odd twist is that after seven years of grueling litigation, nobody was convicted as the leading perpetrator. Still, the high-society Swope family was demoralized and had outlaid more than $100,000 in the legal battles.

The Swope Mansion at this time was headed by the resolute family matriarch, Maggie Swope, who was a daughter of the well-known William Chrisman. Her husband, Logan Swope, had since passed. Their children and Logan's brother, Colonel Thomas Hunton Swope—who had in 1896 donated more than one thousand acres for Swope Park to the people of

Kansas City—lived with the family in the Swope Mansion. Colonel Swope (Colonel was an attribute to wealthy capitalists in those days; he was not a veteran) enjoyed a room in the Swope Mansion as he commuted daily from his office in the New England Building.

Another resident of the home was the beloved elderly family cousin, Colonel (also an attribute) "Moss" Hunton, who was quite popular in Independence social circles.

Colonel "Moss" Hunton died dramatically with terrible convulsions on Friday, October 1, 1909, in the Swope Mansion at Independence. The next day, funeral arrangements were made. But why were *two* coffins ordered from undertaker R.B. Mitchell of Ott & Mitchell Furniture and Funeral Home? Coincidentally, on the following evening, Sunday, October 3, the wealthy businessman and benefactor Colonel Thomas Swope died in a similar manner as Hunton—in the same house.

Profile of Colonel Thomas Hunton Swope. *Courtesy Jackson County Historical Society 004887M.*

Dr. Bennett Clark Hyde, September 13, 1904. *From the Strauss Peyton Photographic Studio Collection. Courtesy Jackson County Historical Society 008881L.*

The twist of events that transpired over the next couple of months would add up to what looked suspiciously like murder, and one of the family's own, Dr. Bennett Clark Hyde, became the controversial suspect. Hyde was the husband of one of Logan and Maggie Swope's children, Frances, who was an heir to a massive fortune that was, by the way, made even more robust with each passing heir.

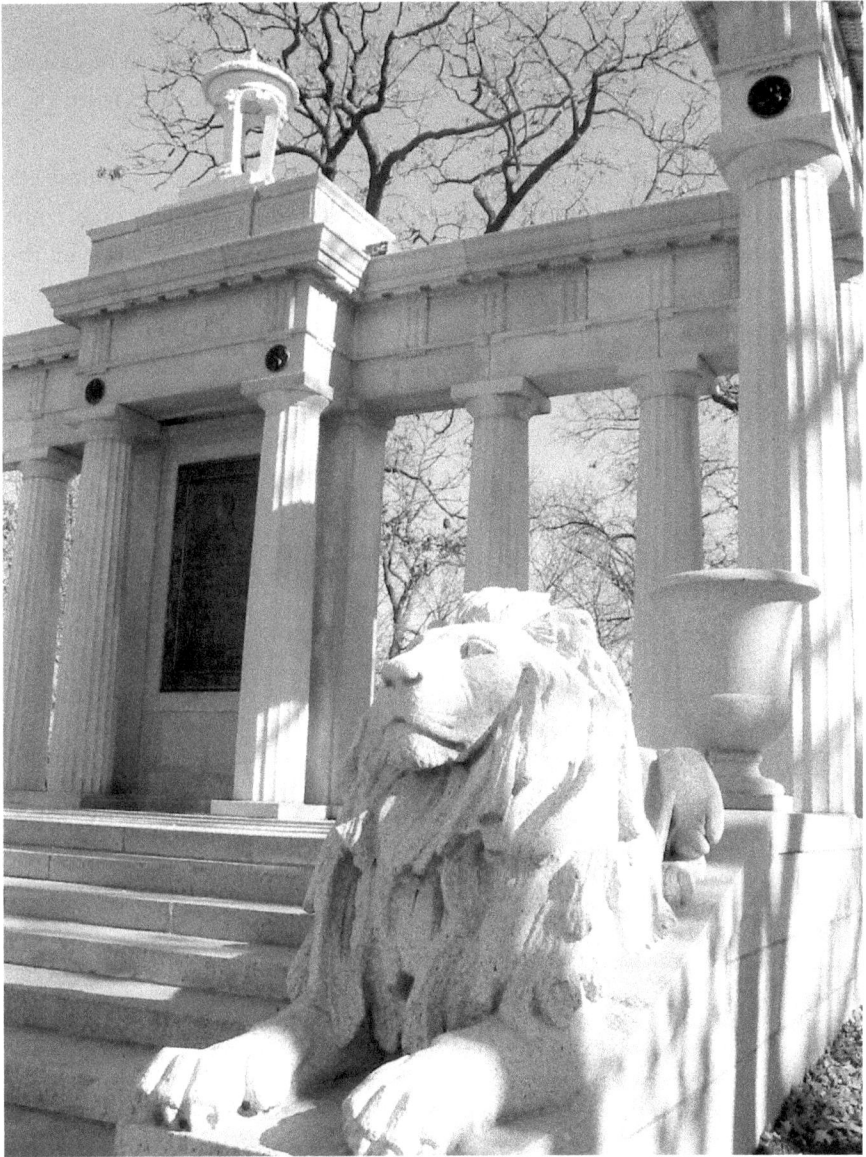

The Colonel Thomas Hunton Swope Memorial overlooking the Big Blue River Valley in Swope Park. *Courtesy the author.*

The 1910 murder case surrounding the wealthy Swope family of Independence, Missouri, gripped newspaper readers throughout the nation: gruesome autopsy reports, outstanding testimony of questionable medical practices, details of suspected murder and mayhem. Fowler's mystery recaps these details exploring the still-unanswered question: was Hyde a diabolical villain bent on inheriting Swope's millions or the unfortunate victim of a family grudge?

Fowler delivers an engaging and accurate retelling of these one-hundred-year-old events in the literary journalism tradition by analyzing court transcripts, newspaper coverage and personal memoirs. To take in the scenarios based on modern science, revisit the dark hallways of the Pleasant Street Swope Mansion in 1909 and judge for yourself. Was it murder?

A Half Century of Triumphs Over Challenges (1926-1976)

Andrew Drumm's March to Make Life Better

Preservation of local history and heritage is a core value for any civic-minded resident. Scores of area nonprofit organizations striving to fulfill that vital role need your support, including the Jackson County (Missouri) Historical Society.

Another local organization, the Andrew Drumm Institute, is worthy of your attention, not only for its goal to save a part of our shared cultural, historical landscape but also for the center of services it provides to area foster children and foster families today.

Drumm Farm, its former brand, was founded through an endowment established by the last will of Major Andrew Drumm, who died in San Antonio while attending the Texas Cattlemen's Association, on April 14, 1919, at the age of ninety-one.

Desiring a home, working farm and vocational training program for disadvantaged youth, Drumm bequeathed $1.8 million to establish the Andrew Drumm Institute, which opened in 1929. For years, Drumm was highly decorated at agricultural and livestock shows, as well as in public speaking and parliamentary procedure contests. In more than seven decades, hundreds of Drumm graduates have become proud alumni and moved on to raise their families with the values and character they formed at Drumm Farm. William W. "Bill" Richards, a 1948 Drumm graduate from

The Andrew Drumm Institute campus, as it looked in the 1950s. Mr. Berkemeier photo album; gift of William W. "Bill" Richards, 1948 Drumm graduate. *Courtesy Jackson County Historical Society 011768NL.*

Oak Grove, has ensured Drumm's history is preserved by depositing original Drumm-related materials in the Jackson County (Missouri) Historical Society's archives.

Andrew Drumm, who was born on February 6, 1828, in Muskingum County, Ohio, rushed to California's gold rush as a forty-niner and mined for gold for twenty years. He then went into the cattle business, eventually becoming a millionaire. In the 1870s, Drumm owned forty thousand cattle. He had ranches in Texas, Oklahoma, Kansas, California, Missouri, New Mexico and Arizona. A clerk in a Wichita store started calling him "Major," and the name stuck. Cattle barons often gained military titles like "Major" or "Colonel" as befitting one commanding respect. At age fifty-eight, Drumm married Cordelia Green, twenty-one years his junior. Mrs. Drumm left another $750,000 to Drumm Farm in her estate when she died in 1937. Both rest eternal in Forest Hill Cemetery.

In 1912, Drumm purchased a 370-acre farm from Alexander Frazier for $85,000 at what is today 3210 Lee's Summit Road. On the property was a three-story brick residence built between 1881 and 1884, which stands today as the Drumm Institute's moniker building, named Swinney Hall (after E.F. Swinney). It contains twelve rooms, eight fireplaces, hardwood floors and eleven-foot ceilings. Originally, the residence had running water made possible by gravity flow; water was pumped up to a water tower and flowed into a storage tank, which is no longer standing. The original slate roof was covered in the 1960s after being damaged by a hail storm.

In 2010, the Drumm Institute began restoring historic Swinney Hall to increase the number of children it may help, improve its program spaces and upgrade facilities to improve efficiency and accessibility.

Keep alive the meaning behind Andrew Drumm's example as you consider supporting a local, nonprofit history and heritage organization like the Jackson County (Missouri) Historical Society.

DISNEY'S WORLD OF HOLLYWOOD ANIMATION FIRST SKETCHED IN KANSAS CITY

When Elias Disney moved from Marceline to Kansas City, Missouri, in 1911, who could have dreamed his nine-year-old son would eventually put Kansas City on the map as the birthplace of Mickey Mouse? Inventive Walt Disney was destined to make sure his exhilarating childhood might be accessible—even through fantasy and make-believe—to children all over the world for generations to come.

At age fourteen, Walt attended classes at the Kansas City Art Institute. Disney's inspiration for the modern theme parks we enjoy today came from Kansas City's own Electric Park (located near Disney's neighborhood at Forty-second and Troost Avenue), featuring shows, dining, roller coasters, log flume rides, miniature trains and other novelty entertainment. Equally tantalizing and influential were Kansas City's theaters booking silent motion pictures and live, vaudeville acts.

After serving nine months in Europe with the Red Cross Ambulance Service during World War I, Disney returned home and became an artist for the Pesman-Rubin Advertising Agency, where he met Ubbe Iwwerks. In 1920, Disney and Iwwerks joined A.V. Cauger's Kansas City Slide Company, which created advertisements on glass slides for theaters to project on screens between films and acts.

Disney learned the process of animating drawings and, at age twenty, incorporated Laugh-O-Gram Films, Inc., on May 23,1922. Laugh-O-Gram artists, operating on the second floor of the McConahy Building on Thirty-first and Forest, produced work comparable to New York's best animated films. Its first series of cartoons, several of which still exist, ran in theaters here and in Europe.

Laugh-O-Gram also created films featuring live-action actors interacting with cartoon animals. With imaginary animal cartoons running through his mind, it is fitting that Disney, who often slept in his studio at night, would befriend a pet mouse. Mortimer took food from Disney's hand, played on his drawing board and later became the inspiration for the world's most-recognized fictional character!

Disney's last Kansas City film was *Alice's Wonderland*, featuring himself and four-year-old Virginia Davis, who meets the owner of a struggling film studio trying to come up with a new idea for a film series; she visits his studio and interacts with animated characters.

Desiring to be closer to family, Disney closed Laugh-O-Gram and moved to Los Angeles, California. He boarded a train at Union Station with forty dollars and his one-reel *Alice* cartoon. Disney's contract for the *Alice Comedies,* October 16, 1923, marks the Walt Disney Company's date of origin. The men who worked with Disney in Kansas City joined him in California. All became pioneers of the Hollywood animation industry.

The success of Disney's first feature-length animated film in 1937, *Snow White and the Seven Dwarfs*, allowed him to purchase land in Burbank, California, that remains Walt Disney Company's headquarters. Disney's achievements eventually won thirty-two Oscars—more than anyone else in motion pictures.

In 1955, Disney opened Disneyland, the world's first theme park. In 1965, he announced his plans to build an even larger complex of amusement parks and a model city, "Epcot," in sunny Florida. Walt Disney died the next year, but his brother, Roy, who had made a promise to his little brother, made sure Walt Disney World opened in 1971; Roy died three months later.

Kansas City's Laugh-O-Gram Films studio (the McConahy Building) is being restored. But public support and a little Disney magic are needed so the nonprofit, Thank You, Walt Disney, Inc., may one day showcase how Disney's world of Hollywood animation was first "sketched" in Kansas City.

The Jackson County Historical Society accepts donations of original photographs, documents, artifacts and memorabilia relating to Disney's life and work in Kansas City to help commemorate the birthplace of Mickey Mouse.

CIVILIAN CONSERVATION CORPS
RELIEVED A GREAT DEPRESSION

During the Great Depression of the 1930s, more than three million single men between the ages of eighteen and twenty-five were inducted into the Civilian Conservation Corps (CCC, or 3Cs). Kansas City native Roy Weldon Jackson was among those ranks. He recalled his year in the 3Cs in the first manuscript on this topic donated to the Jackson County (Missouri) Historical Society.

The CCC was part of Roosevelt's New Deal to help citizens find meaningful employment, active from 1932 to 1942. The Department of Labor was responsible for enrolling eligible men on a state-quota basis, determined by population. The CCC carried out conservation projects worth $1.5 billion.

Like for others of his generation, times were hard, and Jackson was shifted from one relative to another as a child. His mainstays were his paternal grandparents, Arthur and Ida Jackson.

Roy Weldon Jackson said:

> *I turned 18 on August 13, 1936. The month before, I had visited the Kansas City Relief Committee's, Missouri Relief Commission's recruitment office at 125 East 31st Street, to complete my application for a six-month enrollment into the emergency conservation work program. I was out of work and needed a home.*
>
> *On April 5, 1937, I packed a small bag of clothes and the brownie camera my Uncle Reg had given me for my 18th birthday, and went by train from Kansas City's Union Station to Ft. Leavenworth, Kansas. A four-day enrollment process included getting assignments and inoculations. I was to get $30 each month, and $25 would be sent home to my Grandmother (she ended up saving my allotments, some of which I used when I came home to buy a car.).*
>
> *I was...transferred to...Sebastopol, California, located about 11 miles west of Santa Rosa. We assisted the California State Conservation Department in making water irrigation canals (to prevent soil erosion) in the Gold Ridge apple orchard region. I used a pick and shovel, and helped lay the concrete pipes that enrollees also made in the Camp. We also fought forest fires; one fire was in a petrified forest.*

Civilian Conservation Corps enrollees at work in apple orchards in Sebastopol, California. Standing in the drainage ditch at the right is Kansas Citian Roy Weldon Jackson, grandfather of the author. *Courtesy Jackson County Historical Society 012782DS.*

The CCC camps were run like the Army as far as routine and discipline went, but you didn't have to salute. We were awakened by the bugle's call… and they played Taps when lowering the flag at the end of each day. We had military-style clothes, rations, and barracks.

But, we had fun, too. We horsed around and played endless practical jokes on one another…a bucket of water perched above a door…a footlocker pulled out in the aisle to trip an unsuspecting guy on his way to the latrine in the middle of the night. One time the fellas sprinkled Post Toasties in between my sheets. Little did they know, I slept on top of the sheets to stay cool.

Figuring he had it made in sunny Sebastopol, Jackson took advantage of the opportunity for a second CCC enlistment. However, to his surprise, after signing on the dotted line, he was transferred to Coolin, Idaho, "a town real near the Canadian border with three houses, one converted to a bar." Jackson completed his second, six-month enlistment at Camp Drysdale working on conservation projects through the winter in the St. Joe National Forest. He was discharged and returned to Kansas City through Union Station in March 1938.

WINDING THE CLOCK FOR JACKSON COUNTY'S TWO NINETEENTH-CENTURY COURTHOUSES

With the historic Independence Courthouse Square's boutique shops enjoying revitalization in 2010 and the old county courthouse terraces restored to their 1933-era beauty, it is "high time" to "wind the clock" on the history of Jackson County's illustrious Independence and Kansas City courthouses.

More than one-third of Missouri's 114 counties boast courthouses over one hundred years old, representing the most architecturally significant building in their county at the time of construction.

Jackson County has the rare distinction of claiming not one, but *two* surviving nineteenth-century courthouses. J. Bradley Pace, past president of the Jackson County (Missouri) Historical Society and author of *Survivors: A Catalog of Missouri's Remaining 19th Century County Courthouses*, said, "There can be no doubt that they are today among the county's most tangible links with its past."

Though most recently remodeled nearly seventy-five years ago under the planning and supervision of Harry S Truman, then presiding judge (akin to today's county executive) of the Jackson County Court (akin to today's county legislature), the landmark Jackson County Courthouse on Independence Square, listed in 1972 on the National Register of Historic Places, contains remnants from five earlier courthouses dating to 1836.

Immediately after the 1827 log Jackson County Courthouse was erected, construction of a more permanent brick and stone courthouse began that year. Though completed in 1831, the building was improperly constructed and suffered maintenance problems from the start, according to available records. The structure foundered, and the county court ordered construction of a completely new building that was finished in 1836.

Entombed behind the marble walls of the current structure's central lobby and the paneling of the second-floor courtroom stands the two-foot-thick walls of this 1836 two-story, two-room, brick building. A corner closet in the former marriage license bureau was once one of four original, tall fireplace flues at each corner of that building. In the basement, you can still see a brick-lined tunnel from this first structure.

A tall, thin, sharp-pointed spire added in 1846 (the year the ill-fated, 250-wagon Donner party left Independence Square for California) was visible for miles in every direction on the pioneer landscape for the next six years. Of course, it didn't hurt that Independence Square is located on high ground.

Though commonly recorded that Mexican War veterans returning to Jackson County in 1848 found the courthouse enlarged in all four directions and newly resurfaced into a modified Greek Revival style popular at that time, county court records document this enlargement taking place between June 1852 and May 1853. The balanced, symmetrical façade included columned entry porches on the north and south and evenly spaced, simple pilasters projecting slightly from all four walls. The wooden fence previously enclosing the quarter acre was removed. A stunted, domed cupola atop a low-pitched hip roof replaced the prominent 1846 spire. Forty-niners rushed by this courthouse posthaste for gold in California. Its walls quartered soldiers and endured bullets fired in Civil War battles that raged through Independence Square.

A burgeoning postwar reconstruction boom necessitated larger quarters for Jackson County government. In 1872, the first Jackson County Courthouse

Jackson County Truman Courthouse on historic Independence Courthouse Square in Independence, Missouri. *Courtesy Jackson County Historical Society 000188L.*

was constructed in Kansas City at Second and Main. Ever since, Jackson County has had two county courthouses.

Fifteen years later in 1887, additional remodeling included a $35,000 annex built adjacent on the west, connected by an iron bridge from the second floor. In Kansas City that same year, construction began on a new county courthouse that took up the city block between Fifth and Missouri and Oak and Locust Streets. Patterned after the statehouse in Denver, it was opened in 1892.

In 1897, the Independence County Courthouse had a new timepiece installed, plus a bell salvaged from a Missouri riverboat.

In 1907, $100,000 in general revenue funds helped to raise and restyle the building once again. The 1907 courthouse on Independence Square served Jackson Countians twenty-five years until they, at the beginning of the Great Depression, passed a multimillion-dollar bond issue that allotted $200,000 for a new county courthouse on the square. The bond issue also allowed for the construction of a new, twenty-eight-story, $4 million county courthouse in Kansas City, among numerous other public works.

Dedicated by Harry S Truman on September 7, 1933, the new building in Independence incorporated significant remnants from prior remodels back to the original 1836 brick courthouse.

During the remodeling, county court sessions were relocated to the 1828 log courthouse, which had been restored in 1916.

Pace described the end result of the 1933 remodeling as "a pleasing and elegant structure inspired by Independence Hall and resembling a Colonial Virginia meetinghouse."

Red colonial brick and white Indiana limestone trimmings punctuate classical columns and porticos on north and south. Above the east and west entrances are stone reliefs of an American eagle surrounded by a symbolic wreath of victory and progress. The seal of the State of Missouri can be found above the north portico, and the seal of Jackson County above the south portico.

The grounds feature selected monuments and statues of interest, including a west-facing equestrian statue of Andrew Jackson, Jackson County's namesake, presented to Jackson Countians by Harry S Truman upon his election as president of the United States in 1949. A statue of Truman himself on the east end was dedicated May 8, 1976, by President Gerald R. Ford (the equestrian statue was originally situated here and moved to the west side for Truman's statue). Other markers commemorate Jackson County pioneers, the Santa Fe Trail and the Oregon–California Trails and Civil War battles, all of which came through Independence Square from the 1820s to 1860s.

The building, no longer used as a hall of justice or government, will be adaptively reused as a visitor welcome center. Pace quoted travel expert Arthur Frommer, who said, "Tourism does not go to a city that has lost its soul." Pace added, "The Square—and the Courthouse in particular—are certainly a big part of the soul of Independence and Jackson County."

"Wind the clock" today (a saying used by teenagers in the 1930s through 1960s who cruised one way around the courthouse square), patronize renovated boutiques, enjoy the courthouse and grounds and give thanks to those who strive to keep this building relevant. The 1827 log Jackson County Courthouse is also open for tours.

LOST AMERICANA RETURNS HOME

When reading in the *Kansas City Star* ("For many items Americana, it's out with the old," April 10, 2008) about the Hallmark Cards, Inc., auction of Jerry Smith's antique toys and collectables, I recognized one of two cigar store Indian statues being auctioned as significant to Kansas City. I was "a day late and a dollar short" since the auction had already taken place by the time I was clipping the article for the Jackson County (Missouri) Historical Society's newspaper subject files.

The cigar store Indian, once as frequently seen as barber poles, is nearly extinct. Clothed in fringed buckskins, draped with blankets, decorated with feathered headdresses and sometimes shown holding tomahawks, bows, arrows and spears, cigar store Indians were once a universal symbol.

The recent specimen on the auction block was described as a "painted carved wood figure on original tin covered with wood trimmed base with cast iron wheels." A "tin panel on base retains the tobacconist's trade name, 'E.J. Reardon'" cigars and tobacco.

There he was! This was the scout who, for more than fifty years, identified the Reardon Tobacco Company at 709 Main Street in downtown Kansas City. The Reardon Indian was made in Germany and was posted on his sentry duty in 1889. Sometime around 1900, "a passing herd of Longhorn steers knocked off his arm and trampled it beyond repair. A new one was made of metal and the workmanship was so good that even to this very day you can't tell it's an artificial limb."

E.J. Reardon rejected a $1,500 offer in 1948 for the Indian his father bought in 1889 and named Johnny Swift Wing. Ed Reardon, grandson of E.J. Reardon, said Johnny eventually sold and was on display in Crown Center for some twenty years as part of the collection of Kansas City Buick car dealer (and avid collector and philanthropist) Jerry Smith.

Incidentally, in 1974, Smith had also acquired the Indian Hunter (aka Minnehaha) cigar store Indian statue that had for years graced Independence Square. At that time, Smith said, "I have 6 Indians: 5 wooden and 1 pewter. A model imprint cast in pewter uses the same sand mold as a wood carving. Brittle pewter is subject to age-cracks. Five or more paint layers covered 'Indian Hunter.'" The exact whereabouts of Indian Hunter in 2010 remains a mystery. By 1974, it was on loan to Lamar Hunt, and it stood in his offices at Arrowhead Stadium.

Cigar store Indian on the south side of Independence Courthouse Square in Independence, Missouri. *Courtesy Jackson County Historical Society 007368M.*

Smith, who died in 1984, collected for more than twenty-five years and amassed more than eleven thousand antique toys and unique Americana. His greatest joy was exhibiting this amazing treasure-trove as a natural fundraiser to help local charities.

In 1977, Hallmark Cards, Inc., purchased the mammoth Smith collection to use as resource material for its products. It also sold selected items through retail sales at Halls in Crown Center. As noted above, the remainder of the famous collection was recently auctioned.

I e-mailed the auction house, Noel Barrett, who swiftly forwarded my inquiry to the winning bidder who phoned me. It turns out I was *way more* than a dollar short. While another cigar store Indian from Smith's collection went for $70,000, Kansas City's Reardon Indian commanded $22,000.

The best news for Kansas Citians is that Jerry Smith's daughter and son-in-law held the highest bid, and I'm happy to report that the Reardon Indian will be "keeping close to the reservation"; it's now back in Kansas City in the family's private collection.

If you know the whereabouts about the Indian Hunter (aka Minnehaha) cigar store Indian statue that once stood on the sidewalks on Independence Square, please let the Historical Society make a record of it.

It probably isn't politically correct, but it would be worth exhibiting—if even for a short time—these unique statues of Americana so more people might discover their fascinating history. If anything, I would hope it might raise awareness of the importance of preserving artifacts from our local history so they may be available to the public into the future.

Mary Minor Laird's Climb to the Tower

Mary Graham Minor was encouraged by her mother to begin practicing the piano at home at the age of seven. A next-door neighbor's daughter was a dance teacher at the Kansas City Conservatory of Music for Martha Flaugh. Soon, Mary had given up piano for dance lessons at the conservatory. Her mother hoped this training would lead Mary to one day become a dance teacher. Little did she know what the next few years would have in store for her *adorable* daughter.

Mary continued taking dance lessons at the Flaugh-Lewis School of Dancing. Miss Martha Flaugh and her husband, Robert Lewis Jr., operated

The first Tower Line known then as Ernie Rayburn Girls and later Tower Adorables, pictured here on opening day, Friday, April 13, 1934. *Landon and Mary Graham (Minor) Laird Papers; gift of Mary Laird. Courtesy Jackson County Historical Society 012039L.*

the school located on the second floor at 4050 Main Street (across from St. Paul's).

Mary graduated high school in 1930 and was booked by Jack Reid to dance with other girls at food and auto shows in Kansas, Oklahoma and southern Missouri. By September 1930, Mary had enrolled at Kansas City Junior College located at Eleventh and Central in downtown Kansas City. However, she sold her books within two weeks to join the act of Don Valerio and the Diaz Sisters, who were finishing out an R.K.O. tour. At the end of 1933, Mary started dancing for Paul Cholet in his twenty-five-person Coco-Nut Grove Revue, which included singers, comedians and a "beauty chorus."

Mary's parents desperately wanted her to come home off the road and find a "legitimate" job. They would have to wait a few more numbers for this to happen.

Mary was invited by a girlfriend to see Kansas City's Tower Theater after-hours. Mary discovered that there was immediate need of a replacement dancer in the Tower Adorables line. She found herself trying on costumes with the wardrobe mistress and walking through steps with the line captain. The house singer and the Judy Conrads orchestra were rehearsing the acts for the new show opening the next day, Friday, February 22, 1935. Mary performed three numbers that day—in a "legitimate" theater.

The Tower Adorables opened and closed every stage show and danced one big production number in the middle. There were four shows every weekday (five shows on Saturdays and often five Sundays). The line of dancing girls, who often used lots of props, was equal to the Radio City Rockettes, except for its smaller numbers.

Over the next five years, theatergoers would often read "Mary Graham Minor" on the Tower Theater's marquee.

The Great Depression and the decline of vaudeville entertainment took a toll on Kansas City theaters. Many shut their doors permanently. Small, silent motion-picture houses in neighborhoods began to replace the once-thriving downtown live performance theaters. In an attempt to continue operating these theaters, they began offering motion pictures in addition to their live vaudeville acts. By 1939, the Tower Theater was the only combination house.

Mainstreet Theater with Mary Graham Minor Girls on the marquee. *Landon and Mary Graham (Minor) Laird Papers; gift of Mary Laird. Courtesy Jackson County Historical Society 011989AX.*

Mary continued at the Tower Theater until "the bitter end," as she put it. The Tower Theater closed for the second and last time for live performances in December 1940. Coincidentally, the Mainstreet Theater, which had been closed since 1936, reopened shortly after the Tower Theater closed. The Mainstreet was located on the southwest corner of Fourteenth and Main. In just six short weeks, however, the Mainstreet Theater closed its doors again. (The Mainstreet Theater reopened again in 1949 as the Missouri Theatre.)

In March 1947, Mary Graham Minor married Landon Laird after a lengthy courtship. Landon was a columnist and dramatic editor for the *Kansas City Times* (and later the *Star*). He had originated and continued to write the "About Town" column for many years.

Mary finally secured that "legitimate job" after the Mainstreet Theater closed.

Tower Adorable Mary Graham Minor-Laird donated the papers of Landon and Mary Graham Minor-Laird to the Jackson County (Missouri) Historical Society, a collection of scrapbooks and numerous photographs, sheet music, theater programs and other items that relate to their careers in the Kansas City entertainment business during the 1930s and 1940s.

JACKSON COUNTY'S AGRARIAN PAST AT CEDAR CROFT

Lee's Summit Road (once affectionately known as Hereford Boulevard) south of 40 Highway affords travelers with winding, beautifully rounded knolls crested with giant trees. Grace Farrington Gray, writing for the *Farmer's Wife* magazine in 1929, highlighted a "dream in cream and terra cotta red" on the west side of the road just north of Woods Chapel Road: historic Cedar Croft set back behind stone gate posts.

When there was a great demand for more beef breeding cattle during World War I, one of the country's greatest producers was here in Jackson County, Judge Walter Lee and Verda Florence (Thrailkill) Yost. Married in April 1896 in Holt County, Missouri, they came to Kansas City in 1898. Yost, employed by the Byers Brothers Livestock Commission Company, was one of the founders and early presidents of the American Royal, with his wife's inaugural ball gown having been donated to the American Royal Museum.

A Half Century of Triumphs Over Challenges (1926–1976)

The Yosts lived in town at 3207 Benton Boulevard in Kansas City as late as 1910, but their hearts yearned to return to the picture of the farm of their childhood days. Cedar Croft was born in 1911, and by 1919, the Yosts relocated to their country estate after spending two years building the fine home you see today.

Mrs. Yost's home (and her homemaking skills) "put the glow into glorious," according to Gray, who provided a detailed tour of the country home and farm. The once 640-acre tract had a group of great Jersey dairy barns, two 165-ton silos, tenant houses and the Yost home, the lawn of which was thickly planted with cedars, maples and ornamental shrubbery with clumps of peonies and beds of iris.

For the first quarter of the twentieth century, the Yost name was coupled with the social elite of the beef cattle cult, and the tiers of prize ribbons at their farm home re-echoed the praises of Yost Herefords from prize rings all over the country. In 1926, the Yost herd consisted of 175 head at its height, with 60 breeding cows. It may sound strange to us "city slickers" of today, but these were the kings and queens of American beef cattle show rings; Hereford aristocrats, if you will.

Yost also went into partnership with G.H. Olson, a Jackson County pioneer dairyman since 1899. Olson and Yost Dairy produced under the

Mr. and Mrs. Yost's Cedar Croft on present-day south Lee's Summit Road, as pictured in the publication *Opportunities and Resources of Jackson County, Missouri.*

label Cedarcroft Jersey Farm. Three hundred acres of Yost's bluegrass were set aside for cattle grazing for at least seven months of the year; the remainder of the tract was devoted to the production of hay and grain crops. In 1926, Cedar Croft was one of few dairies in the county using milking machines. It produced 150 gallons of Jersey milk daily with its initial herd of seventy-five young Jersey cows (half of which were purebred).

The stock market crash of 1929 and the Great Depression affected Yost's Cedar Croft operations. Though it recovered during the early years of World War II, its property dwindled to 160 acres.

Besides the legacy of Cedar Croft, perhaps Mr. and Mrs. Yost's finest tribute is that they gave home and education to young people who otherwise may not have had either. Though they never had children of their own, they helped several children through school, taking all of them into their home as members of the family.

One of those, Rose Mae Carroll, lived with the Yosts for sixteen years starting at the age of fourteen in 1926 to 1942, when she married Robert Henry Cook. Their son, Walter Lee Cook, of Harrisonville, is named after Mr. Yost. Rose taught at the Oakland School no. 61 from 1932 to 1946, when the country school was closed and consolidated into the Lee's Summit School District. Oakland School house, which still stands today at the corner of Seventy-fifth Street and Lee's Summit Road, was built in 1884 on one acre donated by John W. Kerr the year before.

Yost was later associated as a banker with the Farmers and Merchant's Bank on Independence Square. And he was elected as the Eastern District judge on the Jackson County Court in 1943 and 1945. Mrs. Yost died on January 14, 1945; Mr. Yost on December 11, 1948. They are buried in Mount Moriah Cemetery.

Cedar Croft, remodeled by Drew Hood, is the gem of the neighborhood available to the next lucky caretaker. The fate and sustained, natural beauty of the surrounding neighborhood are the resident's next task.

VETERANS' DAILY LIFE STORIES COLLECTED

April 15 reminds us of the two certainties in life: death and taxes. We avoid talking about both. In regard to the former, it hardly seems fitting that the many veterans eulogized in our daily newspaper remembrances have their loyal service to country truncated to only a sentence or two.

There is a remedy, and it requires veterans and civilians to *act now*. Veterans are hereby enlisted to share their recollections.

Local author (and World War II veteran) Edward T. Matheny Jr. was inspired to write his book, *Pursuit of a Ruptured Duck: When Kansas Citians Went to War*, after reading this call to duty:

> *As veterans of World War II "take their liberty" of this world, what they have lived through and experienced in one of the most eventful times of our country, and of the world, will be lost to us forever unless it is set down and recorded. We need to be about the business of capturing as much of their experience as possible in the short time left to us to do so.*

The Jackson County Historical Society is gathering written and oral history interviews of local veterans from all wars and others who supported wartime activities (such as war industry workers, USO workers, flight instructors, medical volunteers, etc.) through the Veterans History Project. The Library of Congress (LOC), through its American Folklife Center in Washington, D.C., sponsors the national initiative created by Congress in 2000.

The historical society is a "partner archive," meaning that the interviews conducted in Jackson County will be preserved and made available locally.

With the dedicated assistance of volunteers, the historical society has surpassed a benchmark of one thousand oral history interviews of metropolitan Kansas City–area veterans. It is because of local residents' volunteerism that the project functions successfully, and it will continue so long as volunteers contribute their time and talents to this worthy cause. Volunteers also provide their own equipment and supplies because funding appropriations for fieldwork are nonexistent.

The historical society is doing all it can to coordinate this massive project; to make sure that the complexities and intricate details are properly organized; and to ensure the long-term preservation and access of the information and memorabilia being gathered.

Collaborations with other local individuals and entities help spread the message and share the workload, including Gary Swanson and Bob Babcock, with Americans Remembered, Inc.; Raytown Historical Society; the City of

Lloyd Victor Campbell, grandfather of the author, World War II and Korean War U.S. Navy veteran. *Courtesy the author.*

The Liberty Memorial. The commemorative brick in the foreground recognizes and celebrates the author's great-grandfather's World War I service. *Courtesy the author.*

Independence through its Veterans History Hall at the Truman Memorial Building; and a small arsenal of volunteers.

This project is not only about gathering battle stories. Moreover, it's about what everyday life was like at a particular time in American history; it's learning about Kansas City women who engaged in defense to produce two-thirds of all the B-25s flown in World War II; it's about neighborhood kids who pitched in collecting newspapers, scrap metal and grease for recycling. What was rationing? The USO? How did soldiers cope daily? How did they keep in touch with their families back home? The list of questions and answers is endless. Let's dialogue now! Leave behind more than a sentence or two about the experiences of the Greatest Generation and succeeding generations who continue to serve.

Volunteers working with the society have collectively gathered nearly one thousand oral history interviews from local veterans and civilians who supported wartime efforts. These stories are permanently preserved in the society's archives, where they will remain accessible for generations to come.

Help collect and make available rich, colorful stories of your fellow citizens. Veterans may submit their own personal memoirs or pair up with an available volunteer to chat about their wartime jobs. Readers might contribute funds to the Jackson County (Missouri) Historical Society to support the continuation of this project. Without volunteers and funders stepping forward, it cannot continue.

WHEN WORLD WAR II PRISONERS OF WAR CAMPED IN JACKSON COUNTY

Can you image that for a time during World War II Jackson County was crawling with enemy soldiers? This was no invasion; rather, these Germans and Italians were part of a national campaign that brought more than 400,000 Axis prisoners of war (POWs) to the United States for internment. More than 15,000 POWs were dispersed between about thirty camps in Missouri between 1942 and 1945. Though only one camp was located in Jackson County at Atherton, Missouri, POW camps were established at Riverside, Orrick and Liberty.

German prisoners working on the potato harvest in Atherton, Jackson County, Missouri. *Gift of Doris Milano. Courtesy Jackson County Historical Society 002228AS.*

POWs worked at labor-intensive jobs for local farmers under light supervision. They were housed in standard U.S. Army field tents inside a five-acre pasture ringed with barbed wire. Overall, they enjoyed an unbelievably risk-free containment. They arrived as enemies but in many cases left as friends or, at the least, with a more positive view of the United States.

A secondary benefit was that POWs in Jackson County replenished the drain on the American workforce during World War II and, in some cases, saved much-needed crops from devastation. Fifty thousand one-hundred-pound bags of potatoes were produced by Italian POWs in 1943, for instance.

The 1944 camp consisted of German prisoners brought in to help with potato crops. Atherton resident Gale Fulghum said, compared to the Italians, the "Germans on the other hand were all business. They were the elite Aryans from General Rommel's Afrika Korps. Some were 'dyed-in-the-wool' Nazis." "Nazis Arrogance Irks Atherton" read the headline in one newspaper article that went on to note the Germans were whistling at local girls.

By 1945, Jackson County potato growers relied on POW labor. The Germans at the Atherton camp that summer had a special visitor one day: "One day we were told to stay in camp and not go to the fields because we were going to have one of the greatest visitors in the United States to see us," said Walter Meier, who worked at Atherton before being transferred to the camp at Marshall, Missouri. "It was President Truman, and we shined up our shoes—really. He only spoke about a minute, but he said, 'the war is over and you'll be going home soon.'"

Shortly after that, the Germans left Jackson County for eventual repatriation to Europe. Though their work was significant—POWs helped harvest between one thousand and twelve hundred railcar loads of potatoes from the 2,500 acres under cultivation in 1945—only faint memories of their time here remain. Anyone with memories is invited to share with the Jackson County Historical Society.

SHERATON ESTATES: KANSAS CITY'S FIRST AFRICAN AMERICAN SUBURB

The memory of Kansas City's civil rights movement of the early to mid-1960s is kept at the forefront by JoeLouis Mattox, who shared some insight into how our area began to walk the walk of nondiscrimination and equality.

Mattox, a Kansas City Landmarks Commission member, and others are beginning a survey that could lead to the Sheraton Estates subdivision being nominated to both the Kansas City and National Registers of Historic Places. I was excited to learn that my own neighbor and native Kansas Citian, Dewey E. Alexander Jr., was one of the founders of Sheraton Estates. I visited with Mr. Alexander, who shared details about his role in the historic, fifty-year-old development.

Sheraton Estates represents Kansas City's first suburban neighborhood marketed to African Americans beyond the confines of what was then called the Central Negro District, which, up to 1956, did not extend south of Twenty-seventh Street.

Alexander graduated from Kansas City's Lincoln High School, earned a degree from Central State University in Ohio and in 1949 began working part time as a sales representative with his friend, Isadore Gross Jr., at Gross Real Estate Co. at 2224 Vine Street. Their clientele was predominantly middle-class African Americans seeking to upgrade the standard of living for their growing families in the midst of the civil rights era with desegregation, elimination of restrictive covenants and the Fair Housing Act, Alexander said:

> *About the only thing that we could find to sell were older homes in older neighborhoods where whites had moved out. I had an incentive to find something new. One day I was driving out 50 Highway and came to an area where housing and development seemed to have skipped. It was a tract that appeared "out in the country." There was a steep hill, partially wooded at its base. I drove up the hill and a farmer was tending to crops near the crest. There was some quarrying going on and there were a couple of caves at the back edge of the tract near the Missouri Pacific Railroad.*

Believing this area would make a fine new residential development, the partners were given an option to buy the property for $1,000 an acre and $1,000 down. They—together with investors Alvin Hurst, a Kansas City jeweler; R.E. Wolf's Tri-City Construction; and builder and developer W.D. Ray—created Aintree Land Company and set out to plat Sheraton Estates. Alexander and his partners ended up platting Sheraton Estates. "We contracted with the Tuttle-Ayers-Woodward Co. engineers to survey for the plat. And the Kansas City–based, nationally acclaimed landscape architecture firm Hare and Hare were contracted with to stake off lots and design landscaping," said Alexander.

Ultimately, Sheraton Estates's seventy acres included 232 residences between Parkway and Fifty-first Street on the north, Fifty-third Street on the south, Jackson Avenue on the west and the Missouri Pacific Railroad right of way on the east. City mayor H. Roe Bartle said:

> *Our plat was approved by the City Council on March 1, 1957. The Sheraton Homes project represents a valuable addition to this city thoroughly in keeping with the pride and satisfaction our citizens have derived in knowing that our residential areas were among the most beautiful in the nation. Permit me as Mayor of the city of Kansas City, Missouri, to extend to those who are a part of the Sheraton Homes project a congratulatory word on this material contribution to the welfare and forward progress of this great city.*

Dewey Alexander Jr. *Courtesy Dewey Alexander Jr.*

When asked what architect designed the homes, Alexander said, "We researched and found Scholz Homes, Inc., [Scholz Design, Inc., today] in Toldeo, Ohio. We went there to see the prefabricated, luxury, model show houses designed by the founder, Don Scholz Sr., and chose his designs." In all, there were twelve completely different, ranch, bi- and tri-level design model homes (with one and two baths). Newspaper articles promoting the

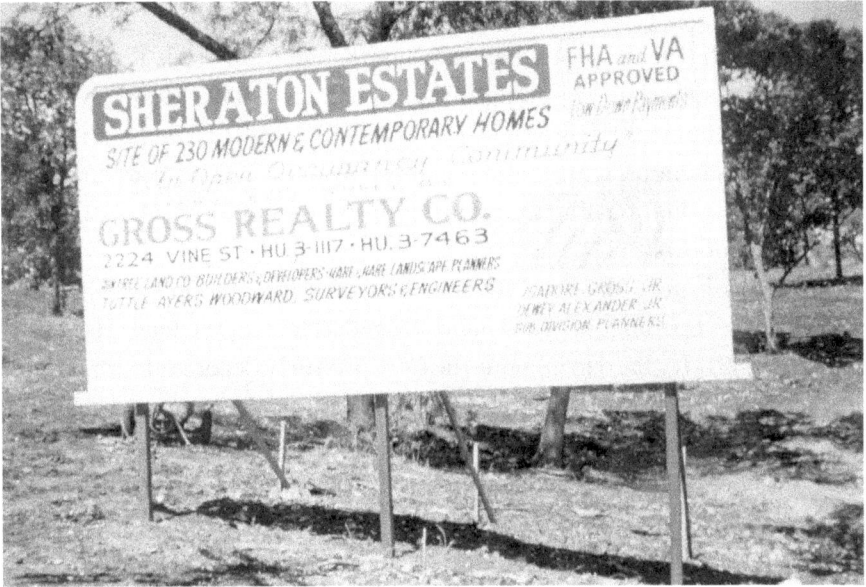

Sheraton Heights construction sign. *Courtesy Dewey Alexander Jr.*

"new homes for modern living" eventually listed the houses from $13,500 to $22,500.

The *Kansas City Star* reported on Sunday, July 14, 1957, that a crowd of twelve thousand people visited the twelve model homes on the day of the grand opening. By 1969, almost all of the lots in Sheraton Estates were built upon. "Many of Kansas City's most celebrated black leaders made—and still make—their home in Sheraton Estates. Sheraton Estates residents continue to be leaders in affecting social and political policy changes that support and improve our community and Kansas City as a whole," said Glenda A. Russell, community organizer for Swope Community Builders.

Above all else, Sheraton Estates paved the way for additional, new "open concept," "non-restricted ownership" subdivisions in Kansas City and Jackson County, Missouri. Thank you, Mr. Alexander and company.

Harzfeld's Dressed Kansas City Elegantly

The next time you may find yourself standing in an aisle at the Walmart Supercenter at Blue Ridge Center, stop for a moment and imagine standing in that same spot when the Blue Ridge Mall—the Kansas City region's first suburban shopping mall—opened in 1958. Mention of the Blue Ridge Mall in 2010 is usually followed with a sigh. To me, Blue Ridge Mall is synonymous with Orange Julius. And as a youngster I always slowed down when passing by sparkly things in Harzfeld's swank fashion boutique windows.

Harzfeld's history dates to 1891 in Kansas City. Hundreds of women attended the opening of Ferdinand Siegel's Parisian's Cloak House in February 1891. It's hard to imagine the store profusely decorated with flowers and plants in the heart of winter. Each lady visitor was presented that day with a bouquet souvenir. Siegel, a member of the big Chicago department store Siegel & Cooper, sold the business to his manager, Siegmund Harzfeld, two years later.

The store had become the largest of its kind in the United States west of New York within fifteen years. In 1906, a $40,000 remodeling was undertaken. The Parisian's five-story building, with 31,250 square feet of floor space at 1008–1010 Main Street in Kansas City, offered a fine assortment of cloaks, wraps, furs and other outer garments for feminine adornment. Initially slated as a $25,000 project, Harzfeld claimed he wanted to attempt "something individual and distinctive."

In December 1913, the Harzfeld Parisian Cloak Company opened on Petticoat Lane a specially built, eleven-story building of cream-colored terra cotta covering a two-block strip of Eleventh Street between Main and Grand.

Harzfeld said:

> *My ambition has been to make Kansas City so much the best place to dress that it will no longer be necessary for the best dressed women in Kansas City to buy their clothing anywhere but in their own town. No longer need the high prices of New York and Chicago, plus the expenditure of railroad fares back and forth, cut into the dress allowance of Kansas City women.*

Joe and Michele Boeckholt, who have been researching Harzfeld's for a number of years, say that in succeeding years Harzfeld's eventually expanded into an adjoining building extending from Main to Walnut Street. The main building at Petticoat Lane has been preserved and was reconfigured in 1986 as part of the Town Pavilion office tower complex.

Harzfeld's window display. *Courtesy Jackson County Historical Society 008195.*

On April 10, 1954, Harzfeld's opened its first branch in Kansas City on the Country Club Plaza. Four years later in 1958, Harzfeld's opened at Blue Ridge Mall, followed by a fourth shop at Corinth Square in 1963 and then Metcalf South shopping mall in 1967.

The Siegel family remained involved in the store's operations. Ferdinand Siegel's son, Lester Siegel Sr., succeeded Siegmund Harzfeld as head of Harzfeld's. Lester Siegel Jr. succeeded his father in February 1966—the store's seventy-fifth anniversary. Allied Stores Corp. acquired the store chain in 1982 and then closed Harzfeld's in 1984.

Ladies—patrons of the bygone, prestigious, specialty fashion and accessory store—may have personal stories—Harzfeld's couture in their wardrobes—yet to share. Did you know Joan Crawford (Lucille Fay LeSueur, who also used the name Billie Cassin) worked as an elevator operator at Kansas City's Harzfeld's?

Gentlemen, too, may have stories relating to Harzfeld's. Independence talent Robert Leroy Smith started out at Harzfeld's art department. He later became a marionette theater owner, manufacturer and teacher of marionette building, playwriting and performance. Upon returning to the area in his later life, he became affiliated with the Puppetry Arts Institute (in the historic Englewood district of Independence, Missouri).

For more details about Harzfeld's history, including its impact on women's fashions and the ready-to-wear industry, visit the Boeckholts' website (http://www.harzfelds.com). Also check out their book *Harzfeld's: A Brief History* from The History Press.

THE PLANNING, PLANTING AND PROPAGATING OF KANSAS CITY'S PARKS AND BOULEVARDS

Kansas Citians today delight in pretty parks and beautiful boulevards—a model for communities across the country. Knowing the winding road our predecessors took to secure these resources might guarantee you value them even more.

The seeds of Kansas City's parks and boulevards system originated in 1872, when J.W. Cook's offer to sell Kansas City forty acres for a park—at a steep $2,000 per acre—was rejected. Cook stewed until 1877, when city newspapers printed the first editorials calling for parks.

Although the city council passed on Cook's renewed offer, it did resolve in 1880 to grade and make the city's first park. Shelley Park was dedicated atop the old, "vacated" City Cemetery, located in the original Town of Kansas between Sixth Street to Independence Avenue and Oak to Locust. Today the highway system has replaced Shelley Park.

William Rockhill Nelson, founder of the *Kansas City Star* in 1880, began advocating for more and larger parks, as well as boulevards. Nelson "planted" letters to the editor, reproduced articles from magazines and newspapers about other cities' parks, had reporters interview visitors and gave ink for local figures to articulate in favor of the idea.

Keep in mind, most of Kansas City was slowly maturing from its "Wild West" beginnings: streets were largely unimproved; city finances were in shambles; and because public improvement bond issues had not passed, there wasn't even a water system. Any public improvement beyond streets and basic needs faced formidable challenges.

After several attempts at charter reform, Mayor Ben Holmes in 1892 appointed a new parks board with the power to issue city bonds. Wealthy Kansas City newcomer August Meyer became the board's first president. Meyer and George E. Kessler, renowned landscape architect, collaborated to create the board's greatest and lasting achievement the following year, their 1893 report, which was summarized and editorialized in the press.

Opponents believed that a park system was expensive and superfluous. As a result, financial, legal and public obstacles needed resolution for the system to flourish. Kansas City attorney Delbert J. Haff is credited with providing legal counsel throughout this process.

The struggle over the parks became complex, but the *Star*'s humor, agitation, resolutions and less obvious forms of persuasion on behalf of the plan rekindled the public's interest in supporting the parks board and for completing the parks and boulevard system. West Terrace Park, Penn Valley Park and North Terrace Park were won only after contentious debate over eminent domain and condemnation issues.

Expansion and improvement of the system, and the creation of the Keep Kansas City Beautiful movement, continue today. The Kessler Society, a nonprofit parks and boulevard advocacy organization, also perpetuates Kansas City's most respected and well-known landscape architect. The George is an award that the Kessler Society and the parks board give to nominated residents each year in recognition of their efforts to beautify their yards and neighborhoods.

The next time you're enjoying green spaces and scenic drives, think of those whose foresight, tenacity and creativity allowed for your experience—Nelson, Meyer, Kessler and Haff—plus all those who serve on the parks board and Kansas City Parks Department employees who take pride in protecting and projecting a system of parks and boulevards that makes other cities "green with envy."

THE NECK: YESTERDAY, TODAY AND TOMORROW

Independence's hometown hero, Harry S Truman, visited Caruthersville, Missouri, in October 1953. After breakfast at the Top Hat Café, Truman tipped his hat and shared kind words with the staff as he was leaving. Truman suggested to one sixteen-year-old that he "finish high school, and attend

Lincoln University in Jefferson City, Missouri." JoeLouis Mattox followed Truman's advice.

Then, between 1966 and 1968, Mattox took a position with the Land Clearance for Redevelopment Authority (LCRA) of Independence, Missouri. Complying with a residency requirement dictating that he live in Independence was a hurdle since, at that time, African Americans could only live in segregated neighborhoods. Mattox lived for a short time on East Waldo with his former college mate, Herb Branson (an Independence resident, who happened to be Caucasian). He then lived with Mr. and Mrs. Jessie Powell on North Noland Road across the street from William Chrisman High School. Mattox said "the Powells were one of the most respected African American families in Independence."

He worked as a relocation specialist for LCRA, which had opened in 1965 an office in the Northwest Parkway Renewal Area—one of two renewal areas covering a 520-acre section of Independence designated and funded by the federal government for improvement and redevelopment. The Northwest Parkway Renewal Area was located on the south side of 24 Highway and was visible from the newly constructed Harry S Truman Presidential Museum and Library on the north side of the highway.

Roy Johnson in the backyard in 1940. *Courtesy Jackson County Historical Society 008492S.*

Nanny with her charge. *Courtesy Jackson County Historical Society 002729S.*

The area that was once the Neck is today McCoy Park. Bess Truman Parkway runs adjacent to the stream that meanders through the area. *Courtesy the author, with compliments to Heritage House for permission to photograph from its rooftop.*

Mattox was responsible for finding and relocating some 125 Independence residents to decent, safe and sanitary homes that were within their means and in reasonably convenient locations. Part of the Northwest Parkway Renewal Area included a predominantly African American neighborhood locally known as the Neck. Mattox said:

> *In many regards the Neck was a ghetto. The quality of housing in the blighted area designated for renewal was substandard and, in some cases, quite unsafe. Even having come from a very rural community in southern Missouri where one might expect to see shanties and the like, I had never personally seen people living as poorly as they did there. I would not have lived [there], nor would I have wanted my parents to live in such a place.*

A number of families and individuals in the Neck—10 to 15 percent of whom were Caucasian—could trace their descendants back to

Independence's frontier days. Most residents were ordinary, working-class families, many of whom served as maids, cooks and gardeners for well-to-do families in adjacent white neighborhoods. Some were retired, others quite elderly. Jon Taylor provides a succinct overview of the demographics of the population and cultural landscape in his book, *A President, a Church and Trails West*.

Mattox admits that:

> *While the end result was the best for some; for others it was not. People's lives were affected and they endured pain and suffering, which I acknowledge. There are some who see me as having "betrayed the black community" for the work I did. Or, that I was a "token for the white man." Some might equate me to "Uncle Tom." They have the right to their opinion, but I hope they may understand that there was a job to do, and I felt I did it with sensitivity and understanding...I felt then as I do now that my work in community development and historic preservation has meaning.*

Eventually the redevelopment area formerly known as the Neck became Bess Truman Parkway, which today bisects an eighteen-acre McCoy Park south of 24 Highway.

It's time to give thanks to how the quality of life for all Americans has improved over the last fifty-five years since this story originated with Mr. Truman. Mattox describes more about his work in detail with personal recollections in a full-length feature article in the *Jackson County Historical Society JOURNAL*.

Preserving the Past for the Future (1976-2026)

Harry S Truman's Civil Rights Legacy

Though Harry S Truman was raised in an era and environment in which segregation and subordination of blacks were accepted practices and institutions, he challenged the status quo. Though his political mentor's New Deal included the Fair Employment Practices Commission to prevent discrimination in defense industries, race relations in general were largely unaddressed. Upon Franklin Delano Roosevelt's death, President Truman stepped up to the plate.

Years before, Truman ran on a platform of plain and decent ideals embodied by any ordinary citizen. As a Missouri senator in the 1930s, Truman consistently supported legislation to abolish poll taxes and prevent lynchings. He wanted all Americans to have a fair chance at opportunity.

In the years leading up to the famous 1948 presidential election, Truman had been continually challenged by civil rights opponents, and he pushed to bring civil rights to the forefront as a national issue after Supreme Court rulings began to roll back the permissible areas of legal discrimination.

Clark M. Clifford, as special counsel to the president, presented Truman with a forty-three-page confidential memo suggesting the electoral strategy in the upcoming election. Clifford particularly emphasized the importance of the black vote, especially beyond the South.

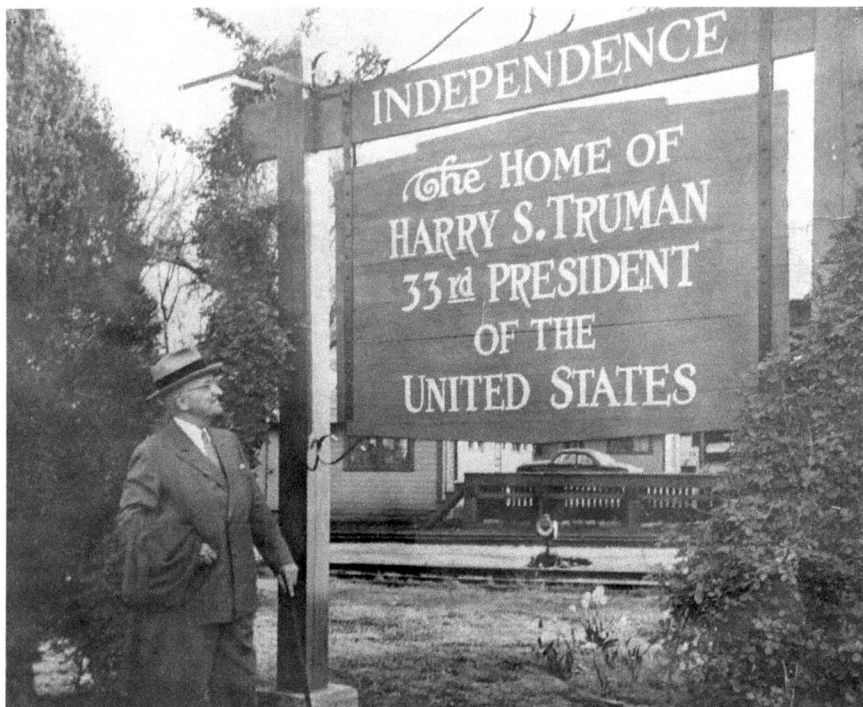

Harry S Truman, the man from Independence and the thirty-third president of the United States. *Courtesy Community of Christ Archives, Truman Library Collection 62-118.*

In June 1947, a Committee on Civil Rights was established. Truman then became the first U.S. president to address the National Organization for the Advancement of Colored People (NAACP), where he declared, "We can no longer afford the luxury of a leisurely attack upon prejudice and discrimination."

The Committee on Civil Rights presented its report, "To Secure These Rights," to the president in October 1947. Reaching beyond its initial instructions to suggest new safeguards against racial violence, the committee pointed out the inequities of life in the Jim Crow South and the rest of postwar America. Truman heralded the report as "an American charter of human freedom" that "will take its place among the great papers of freedom."

Truman's January 1948 State of the Union address promised Congress a special, ten-point civil rights message that eventually solidified civil rights as an important issue in the election that November. Truman took considerable political risk in backing civil rights and had concerns that the loss of Dixiecrat (a term you might look up on Wikipedia) support might destroy the Democratic Party. Still he believed that if he lost the election because of his civil rights platform, it would be for a good cause. Once again, principle mattered more than his own political fate—Truman had the courage of his convictions.

Truman accomplished some of his goals. On July 26, 1948, the president issued Executive Order 9981, bringing an end to racial segregation within the ranks of the United States military forces and forbidding racial discrimination in federal employment. Although most of his reforms stalled in a conservative Congress, by the end of the Korean War in 1953 the U.S. military was almost completely desegregated.

As a result of this and other acts, Truman's contribution to civil rights set the stage for future civil rights progress. Most of all, perhaps, he gave hope and inspired African Americans to *own* the ideals of the American Dream. The Harry S Truman Library and Museum in Independence, Missouri, attracts visitors worldwide who seek to know more about this famous American.

Kansas City Women of Independent Minds

Author and local historic preservationist Jane Fifield Flynn faced a daunting challenge in the early 1990s when researching her book, *Kansas City Women of Independent Minds*. She wanted to provide insights into some of Kansas City's founding mothers—women who had contributed to our area's evolution equal to the men and whose history is well documented.

However, Flynn found scant comprehensive resources about local women and few collected primary materials.

Flynn's frustration was the Jackson County (Missouri) Historical Society's gain. Flynn, who was joined in 1997 by former Independence mayor Barbara J. Potts, then executive director of the historical society, began a noble campaign.

They sought to collect and preserve original materials specifically about individual, local women and women's organizations. The grass-roots effort they began is fueled with each donation to the historical society, where a social history on local women continues to amass.

Jane Fifield Flynn, past president of the Jackson County (Missouri) Historical Society and author of several books, including *Kansas City Style* and *Kansas City Women of Independent Minds*. *Courtesy Jackson County Historical Society 009089M.*

The holdings include the personal, business, social and professional papers of local women in history including, but in no way limited to, pioneers, socialites, artists, teachers, athletes, journalists, homemakers and volunteers from all segments of society.

Women do not have to be famous. The purpose of centralizing a variety of primary records and artifacts is so that researchers may have access to firsthand materials that tell real-life stories of any specific aspect of local history—from women's perspectives.

What are primary records and artifacts? The list is endless, but they often include one-of-a-kind items—letters, memos, diaries, rosters, minutes, badges, certificates, speeches, etc.—that help to document an event or activity of an individual woman, or women's organization, central to Jackson County's history.

Look closely at the details of your daily life (personal, professional, social, extracurricular, etc.). What kind of primary documents, photographs and artifacts might you have assembled or created? What types of materials might you have inherited? Now approach the Jackson County (Missouri) Historical Society with the possibility of donating these so that future generations may have solid, accessible evidence when researching or writing about any aspect of area history.

PROTECT SCENIC VISTAS WHILE THEY LAST

Historic preservation includes more than saving old buildings and operating museums. Protecting landscapes and cultural heritage sites is equally imperative, especially with the swift encroachment of relentless urban sprawl. Shouldn't we reserve the few natural spaces that remain so future generations might enjoy the pristine splendor of an old-fashioned Sunday drive in the countryside?

Consider the scenic and historic Little Blue River Valley along South Noland and Lee's Summit Roads between 40 and 350 Highways and arterial roads. This picturesque valley may be one of the last remaining virtually untouched rural vistas in Jackson County. The valley boasts historic sites and homes, farms, family-owned businesses, sacred burial grounds, pioneer churches and Civil War battlefields. Then there's the stunning views afforded on drives through these wooded hillsides that make this a gem needing to be treasured.

Former Native American paths along the valley predate the earliest European immigrant enclave settling Little Blue, Missouri. An early settler to the area was William Moore, one of a dozen Revolutionary War Patriots who made it as far west as Jackson County. Moore's log cabin beside Ess Road is near his grave site, located east of the Kemper family's Walnut Hill home that overlooks Little Blue (a stately home built by Kansas City lumberman Hans Dierks and later a country retreat of a Kansas City notable named Pendergast).

Infamous Cole Younger's father, Colonel Henry Washington Younger, owned a huge plantation in this area until the Civil War, when Kansas marauders killed him and forced Cole's mother to burn the family home in the dead of winter. Younger's cousin, Armenia (Crawford) Selvey, was one of several Confederate-sympathizing women who died when their Kansas City prison collapsed, triggering William Quantrill and his raiders to burn Lawrence, Kansas. Armenia and two other girls from the prison were buried

A rural eastern Jackson County vista from 1933 worth preserving. Photo by Dick Millard for *Results of County Planning. Courtesy Jackson County Historical Society 009407X.*

in the Davis-Smith Cemetery (intermarrying pioneer families that owned adjoining land). Also laid to rest there are Union and Confederate veterans and another Revolutionary War Patriot, Thomas Starr. Preservationists in 2010 want to mark this historic quarter-acre parcel.

Civil War engagements ravaged this section of the Little Blue River Valley, including a skirmish along White Oak Creek to the south and another on Grinter's farm, at the northwest corner of Lee's Summit Road and Little Blue Road. This tract is just north of present-day Truman Medical Center at Lakewood; the hospital's chronology dates to 1852, when Jackson County established a three-hundred-acre Poor Farm on this site.

After the Civil War, a multitude of livestock and dairy farms established and thrived on the fertile grasses of the valley and lifted the area to world-renowned status in the first part of the twentieth century. W.B. Frey's Lakeside Dairy Farm, surrounding the town of Little Blue, Missouri, was once the world's largest Hereford farm. Jersey cows on Walter Lee Yost's Cedar Croft Farm (along the west side of present-day Lee's Summit Road at Little Blue Road) produced 150 gallons of milk per day. Cedar Croft's residence is restored, but the surrounding property is in jeopardy of being compromised by small-lot subdivision. Four Gates Farm, along Rickey Road, was designed by noted Kansas City architect Mary Rockwell Hook. And Unity Farm sustained people in need through the Great Depression.

Before going to Washington, Harry S Truman in 1934 promoted the reservation of large tracts of Jackson County land for future parks and recreational facilities in a report titled *Results of County Planning*. A current "master plan" for this section of the Little Blue River Valley is in place. But its recommended low-density, large-lot residential areas with open spaces are gradually eroding with each amendment to smaller, denser development.

Will tomorrow's citizens have physical evidence of this historic district's attractions? Before the uniqueness of this area is obliterated forever, this rural landscape is what the people who live on or own land today in the Little Blue River Valley must ally to preserve. Hopefully preservationists, community development leaders, contractors and developers will collaborate with the mindfulness and foresight championed by Harry S Truman when he launched in 1933 his benchmark *Results of County Planning*.

THE JURY IS IN: HOTEL PRESIDENT EXEMPLIFIES KANSAS CITY HOSPITALITY

Kansas City, Missouri's west-facing Hotel President (presently Hilton President Hotel), a twelve-story building on the northeast corner of Fourteenth and Baltimore, opened its doors in February 1926. It was literally at the center of the city's social hub through the 1940s and was widely known for its beautifully decorated dining facilities, cocktail lounges, public spaces and an elegant roof garden that could accommodate 650 people.

Architects Shepard & Wiser incorporated sumptuous artistic decoration and the most modern guest accommodations for 453 guest rooms and 19 private rooms. The hotel boasted a public address system—called a "radiocasting" system—and an ice manufacturing plant that could produce nearly eight thousand pounds of ice each day. The total cost of the initial construction: $2.5 to $3 million.

Hotel President's elaborate architectural elements testify to an opulent period in Kansas City's history. The 1983 National Register of Historic Places nomination application describes the physical appearance of the building in greater detail.

The Hotel President was altered in 1941, 1951 and 1970. Interior "upgrades" included a 1941 cocktail lounge named the Drum Room, complete with a 280-square-foot South Sea Island motif mural by New York artist Winold Reiss (the mural was removed after the hotel closed and is currently in a lounge in New York City). Exterior changes included a light court with a bridge at the upper floors that altered the original rectangular footprint of the building.

The hotel survived until the decline of the downtown Kansas City business district, closing in 1980.

Although it was listed on the National Register of Historic Places in 1983, that did not prevent its near demolition in the mid-1990s. The wrecking ball was thwarted with the advocacy of the Historic Kansas City Foundation. In 2004, the city council approved funding for the rehabilitation of the hotel.

Ron Jury purchased the Hotel President in 2001. Fortunately for Kansas Citians, Jury's work as a developer includes a passion for what historic preservation *really is*. As he puts it, "Historic Preservation is restoring dreams, not just buildings." Jury is intensely interested in recording and documenting individuals' recollections and connections to the Hotel President. One of

Hotel President. *Courtesy Jackson County Historical Society 005379PC.*

many stories he's discovered is that baseball Hall of Fame inductee Lou Gehrig spent his last days in baseball at exhibition games here in Kansas City, and he stayed at the Hotel President. Then one day he went to the Mayo Clinic and never played baseball again. Jury has met former elevator operators and bellmen. In San Diego, California, he happened to meet someone who, just by chance, mentioned that he and his father had been barbers at the hotel the entire time it had been in operation. Another patron also showed Jury a photograph of the front lobby when Gene Autry brought his famous horse into the hotel.

The Jackson County Historical Society seeks to file these stories and attract memorabilia associated with this and other Kansas City hotels (from photographs to hotel restaurant menus and china, silver and stemware) so they may be available to the public into the future.

You can't miss the light bulb–studded "PRESIDENT" sign atop the hotel, once again signaling south that the Kansas City Hilton President Hotel is open for business. The hotel manager would also like you to know there is vacancy!

GROWING NATIVE LANDSCAPES HONOR EARTH, PIONEERS

Anyone interested in minimizing their impact on the environment can begin "going green" by planting native trees, flowers, grasses and sedges. The advantages of planting a diverse variety of hardy, native trees are many, including shade (and lowering utility costs), windbreaks, providing havens for birds and producing oxygen for all animals (this means you). Then there's beautification, including spring flowers and autumn leaves. It's also a return to the natural landscape of our ancestors.

When the first settlers to Jackson County began arriving in growing numbers by the mid-1820s, they selected the site of Independence Courthouse Square as the county seat for its abundance of fresh springs and majestic forest of elm, oak, walnut and hickory where Native Americans had camped for ages. They brought with them heritage roses, iris, lilac, peony, day lily, hollyhocks and yucca.

Early European and Native Americans alike respected the beauty of stately trees; neither felled a tree unnecessarily, which is a stark contrast to the clear cutting that typifies modern development. Founders cut only those trees that had to give way for streets and buildings. Trees so concealed the fledgling Independence Courthouse Square that strangers were unaware of its existence until they came to the clearing in the woods. Abner E. Adair, who was born in Independence in 1832, could remember when the courthouse square was full of stumps. Our forbearers also planted new trees when old growth stands were harvested, so that Independence and Jackson County is still rich with bountiful foliage.

But even trees planted long ago and that have survived the woodsman's ax have a natural lifespan. And external forces like drought, sleet, wind, disease and pests can hasten the demise of these stately treasures.

The current push to "go green" and "grow native" means a reversal of turf (needing continual mowing, weed whipping and edging) to native grasses and sedges. Once their long roots are established, they are drought resistant and virtually maintenance free.

Native flowers are perennial and would be a carefree alternative to the annuals that must be purchased and installed each season. The purple coneflower is the official flower of the city of Independence—and it's a native of our area! Shouldn't every homeowner have a patch?

Perennial flowers and hardy trees that are native to your area should be installed. In Independence, the burr oak is the city's official tree. Since Jackson County is named after Andrew Jackson, a redbud or a variety of southern magnolia like those planted on his Tennessee estate, the Hermitage, would be ideal. The Lewis and Clark expedition could be honored with the planting of any variety of natives they "discovered."

Go green! Respect Mother Earth. Honor your ancestors.

OLD WESTPORT IS THE REAL McCOY

John Calvin McCoy—son of the Reverend Isaac McCoy, who founded the historic Shawnee Mission—made an investment that he soon wished to capitalize upon. In 1833, he built a two-story log building on the northeast corner of Westport Road and Pennsylvania to serve as a business structure and residence. The next year "West Port" was appointed a U.S. post office.

Then, on February 7, 1835, McCoy filed a plat for sixty-two lots that became the nucleus of Westport, Missouri. Santa Fe Trail—and later Oregon–California Trails—travelers outfitting in Independence twenty years thereafter would have the opportunity to enjoy "civilized" society one last time before "jumping off" on their journey west. Remember, the state line up to 1854 was the western edge of the United States, and Westport was the farthest "western port" gateway to the frontier prairie.

Westport became a thriving trading station. Traders following the two-way trail between Westport and Santa Fe, Mexico, exchanged fine goods, staple groceries, clothing and blankets imported from Manchester, England, for Mexican silver ingots. And the furs and buffalo robes of the Shawnee, Delaware, Wyandotte and other Native American cultures were exchanged for goods supplied by European American traders and mercantilists like McCoy and his contemporaries, Alexander Majors and Jim Bridger, who are memorialized today with a larger-than-life statue in Pioneer Park at the intersection of Westport Road and Broadway.

McCoy's next achievement was to convince Missouri River steamboats to continue upriver from Independence and anchor at a landing closer to Westport. This natural rock ledge, located at the base of present-day Grand Avenue, allowed for the transport of supplies and settlers to the edge of the frontier—and much closer to McCoy's Westport community. Paddle your way to the Arabia Steamboat Museum just blocks from this historic spot in the City Market in downtown Kansas City.

A settlement soon formed at the river's edge, and Westport Landing soon became the new Town of Kansas, which McCoy and other investors purchased and incorporated. This town eventually grew into a major metropolitan city—Kansas City.

Westport was incorporated in 1837 when a special charter for the city was obtained.

Thirty years later, the climax of the great attempt of the Confederacy to break the Union defense west of the Mississippi took place on October 21, 1864, with the Civil War Battle of Westport. The fighting began near present-day Forest Hill Cemetery and stretched through present-day Loose Park and into the area of the Country Club Plaza. Imagine 29,500 men in the engagement where 1,000 were killed and several thousand were wounded. A Battle of Westport Museum is operated by volunteers in the main shelter at the entrance to Swope Park.

Westport was eventually incorporated as a fourth-class city in 1881, and A.P. Warfield was elected mayor. However, within fifteen years, Westport ended with its annexation into Kansas City.

Preserving the Past for the Future (1976–2026)

About fifty years after the Civil War Battle of Westport, the Westport Improvement Association resolved in 1912 to hold a weeklong Santa Fe Trail and Battle of Westport Reunion and Carnival. The goal was to obtain funds for a monument in memory of these two "monumental" events. Within days, Westport was abuzz.

The Daughters of Old Westport, a social, historical and memorial organization, was born as part of this occasion. They met at the abandoned Harris House Hotel on the northeast corner of Westport Road and Pennsylvania on August 9, 1912. Interestingly, the Harris House Hotel had been saved from the wrecking ball to be put into service one last time. The reunion and carnival manager's offices were stationed in the hotel. And, during the carnival, luncheons were served in its dismantled dining room where long ago Daniel Boone, Jim Bridger, Kit Carson and other famed frontiersmen often dined.

Wiedenmann Brothers, operating at 500 Westport Road in 1909 in the former Albert Gallatin Boone store, purportedly the oldest surviving structure in Kansas City. *Gift of John and Pat Wiedenmann. Courtesy Jackson County Historical Society 011193S.*

Pioneer Park in the Westport district of Kansas City, Missouri. *Courtesy the author.*

An estimated eight thousand people attended the carnival grounds the first night.

The first annual convention of the Daughters of Old Westport, by then 58 members strong, took place the following year in 1913 when more than

150 "old-timers" of Westport shared firsthand facts and dined together in the Westport Avenue Presbyterian Church.

Over the years, the daughters' contributions to the community have been many. Their crowning achievement, however, might just be the placement and dedication in October 1920 of the granite memorial that still stands in the triangular parcel on Broadway where High and Washington Streets converge; it's dedicated to the "Pioneers of Old Westport" and "To the Pioneer Mother."

Daughters of Old Westport were originally those who were born and reared within the precincts of the famous settlement, had lived there forty years or were descendants of those who made Westport famous in frontier days. Westport Historical Society helps to keep the history of Westport alive at its Harris-Kearney House at 4000 Baltimore, Kansas City, Missouri.

CONSERVING CEMETERIES AS SACRED SPACES

The practice of placing flowers on the graves of soldiers originated as early as 1866 among southern women. General John A. Logan, as commander in chief of the Grand Army of the Republic (an organization of Union veterans), formalized the Memorial or Decoration Day commemoration in 1868. Several congressional acts have led us to the Monday Holiday Law we follow today.

Kansas City observed Decoration Day in May 1880 when C.C. Allen marshaled what became an annual parade. More elaborate services were initiated in 1882 when Major William Warner (later a U.S. senator), who with his mounted staff, led veterans followed by women and children carrying flowers as they marched from Sixth and Wyandotte Streets to Union Cemetery and decorated graves.

Residents of the Kansas City metropolitan area have an opportunity to pay respects to those who have gone before at any number of local cemeteries. There are some three hundred pioneer graveyards scattered throughout Jackson County. A few of the larger, older, municipal cemeteries include the following:

(1) Elmwood Cemetery on Truman Road opened in 1872. Its beautiful grounds were designed by renowned landscape architect George Kessler,

the creator of Kansas City's famed parks and boulevard system. Elmwood encompasses forty-three acres in the heart of Kansas City and is the final resting place for over 36,000 souls from all walks of life, including many of Kansas City's founders. The cemetery offers a historical map and has a great website, http://www.elmwoodcem-kc.org.

(2) Mount Washington Cemetery between Truman Road and Independence Avenue (24 Highway) opened in 1902 (formerly Washington Park proffered by Willard E. Winner). If you haven't toured this cemetery, you are in for a treat. Beyond the sheer beauty of the sacred space, there are magnificent tombs and mausoleums to enjoy. The Emma Long (Mrs. John) Memorial Chapel is being restored. William Rockhill Nelson (founder of the *Kansas City Star*) has a mausoleum that is twice as big as my house. Don't miss famous mountain man Jim Bridger's grave, among others. At this time, we are unaware of a history tour/map, but here is the website: http://www. mtwashingtonforever.com/MtWashington.

Above and opposite: Kunigunde (née Friedricks) (Mrs. Fred) Kruger's Woodmen of the World tombstone in Union Cemetery. Kuni is the author's great-great-great-grandmother. *Courtesy the author.*

ERECTED BY THE
WOODMEN CIRCLE
KUNI
WIFE OF
FRIEDRICH KRUGE
FEB. 21 1843
JULY 18, 1903
AT REST

(3) Union Cemetery's original site was donated in 1857 by Dr. James W. Hunter. The original, picturesque forty-nine acres were situated amid rolling countryside along the first turnpike (or toll road) west of the Mississippi that Westport merchants had constructed between their frontier town (Westport) and its river port landing, the Town of Kansas (north of the City Market today). The original entrance to the cemetery was beside the bustling road

(today Twenty-seventh and Main Streets), where a tollgate charged all north- and southbound travelers. Check out the Union Cemetery Historical Society at http://www.uchskc.org.

(4) Woodlawn Cemetery's earliest burial dates to 1819 (seven years before Jackson County was even formed). Three small local cemeteries were eventually joined together—with additional land purchases—until it reached its current proportions. This city-operated spot is most deserving of your attention and support. Check out the city's parks and recreation cemetery page at http://www.ci.independence.mo.us.

Two books produced by the Jackson County (Missouri) Historical Society might be of assistance to those desiring to locate pioneer graves or to learn how to protect an abandoned graveyard. *Vital Historical Records of Jackson County, Missouri: 1826–1876* is a reprint of a 1934 Daughters of the American Revolution publication, with a new and improved full-name and subject index. The seven-hundred-page book includes extracts of church and cemetery tombstone inscriptions covering the first fifty years of Jackson County, Missouri. Another publication, *Conserving Missouri Cemeteries: Preservation, Statutes and Common Decency*, is an informational booklet that discusses practical ways that individuals, neighbors, neighborhoods and communities may realistically care for small, pioneer cemeteries that are being encroached upon by development.

JACKSON COUNTY COUNTS: COUNTING AMERICA'S STORIES ONE BY ONE

Authors and historians seek *original* materials when researching. Unique, one-of-a-kind documentation is the "stuff" of nonfiction books, museum exhibits, television documentaries, doctorial dissertations, historic building certifications, etc. The types of historical materials are endless. Whether it's a letter from the 1850s, a diary from the 1890s, a telegram from the 1940s or an e-mail from the 1990s, an assemblage of a variety of primary resources is vitally important and valuable to researchers.

We each experience and are a part of history with each passing day. As time ticks, every one of us accrues personal life stories, no matter if we are eighteen, fifty-eight or eighty-eight years old. A few keep detailed, daily journals or diaries, or even letters or e-mails. Others are good at storytelling but rarely seem to write anything down or record their stories on audio- or videotape. Believe it or not, your stories are historical treasures that may be recorded nowhere else. Shouldn't they be preserved?

Now, think of the infinite, varied and diverse perspectives that often vanish when we die. "Wouldn't it be great if Grandma had written about (this or that)?" You don't have to be an elder to record a memory or life experience. In fact, it's best to record an experience as it is happening, in real time. If that isn't possible, then a recollection jotted down some time (even years) after the fact may suffice. Your challenge in any event is to begin writing *something* down—one individual, memorable story at a time. Soon you'll have a collection worth sharing for posterity.

Though most of us think our lives are ordinary and mundane, the extraordinary difference between you, me and the next reader will be the relatively small ratio of us who actually take the time to record and share our firsthand memories. Writing one's "life story," or "autobiography," need not be a chronological reiteration of names, dates and places but rather a collection of random thoughts, feelings and memories—recorded one at a time—and then assembled for posterity. As one memorable early 1970s television commercial advised (promoting a product that I'll let you recall for yourself), "Try it, you'll like it."

Ideally, a firsthand recording of events while they are happening in real time is preferred. However, a memory or recollection prepared after the fact can fill a void whenever firsthand recordings of an event are lacking. The great thing is, everyone has a personal story or stories to tell. The sad thing is, the majority of people fail to transfer them from their minds onto a recordable platform. That is, they rarely write them down or audio- or videotape their stories for posterity.

The Jackson County (Missouri) Historical Society encourages you to dedicate some time to record events important in your life for yourself—for your family—and hopefully for future generations to enjoy and learn from. This is the kind of "stuff" that can never be found elsewhere in recorded history unless *you* write it down and donate it.

It doesn't have to be a lengthy project, and it doesn't have to be "professional." Express your individuality in the way you present your own story or stories.

Think about your daily life experiences, your thoughts and dreams, your favorite memory or memories or how you "fit" into a larger community—and write *something* down.

Harry S Truman. *From the Strauss Peyton Photographic Studio Collection. Courtesy Jackson County Historical Society 018518X.*

Start by writing about just *one* story or experience. Share it with a friend or family member (or get some feedback from a local, historical repository like the Jackson County (Missouri) Historical Society) who may have some questions for you that may help you fill in details you may have taken for granted.

Once you get one story recorded, you'll likely be inspired to record another as your time permits. Before you know it, you may have a collection of random, personal stories (one memory or recollection at a time) that could be quite interesting to your family and also a great value to researchers or historians 50, 100 or 150 years from now.

Take that extra step to deposit your story or stories with a local archive so they may be counted! They'll be preserved; and they'll be made available to the public into the future. You may even have documents, artifacts or photographs that support or complement your story. These could add visually to a particular story.

The Jackson County (Missouri) Historical Society is currently involved in two oral history projects, with the help of volunteer assistance. One is for veterans and civilians who have participated in wartime efforts and is called the Veterans History Project, a program of the American Folklife Center at the Library of Congress. The second is the oral history project of the Gay and Lesbian Archive of Mid-America (GLAMA), which seeks to gather the perspectives and memorabilia of Kansas Citians in that minority group for posterity. There are also local cottage businesses that assist individuals in recording their life's stories. Won't you be counted? Find out more at http://www.jchs.org.

JACKSON COUNTY HISTORICAL SOCIETY'S ILLUSTRIOUS PAST AND GLIMMERING FUTURE

The Jackson County Historical Society (JCHS) first assembled in 1909 for an Independence Day picnic on the shaded lawn of the John B. Wornall House in Kansas City, Missouri. The 1909 celebration was quite a show. In place of the traditional fireworks or a brass band, Kansas City pioneers and their children observed older customs by standing to sing the national songs without accompaniment and by reading the Declaration of Independence. About two hundred people enjoyed the simple ceremonies that day, such as recognizing the attendee of longest residence in the county and listening to poignant speeches about the history their families had helped create. Amazingly, these participants also had the foresight to recognize and envision a great need for "the preservation...[and the] care and exhibition of historic articles and documents relating to Jackson County."

That vision of collecting, preserving and sharing is one that continues today after more than one hundred years. The mission of JCHS echoes that early day call for an unyielding dedication to the preservation and understanding of our county's heritage.

JCHS formally organized January 19, 1940, and ramped up its activity and officially incorporated in 1958 when the oldest structure on Independence Courthouse Square was slated for demolition—the 1859 Jackson County Jail and adjoining Marshal's Home. After a fervent capital campaign under the leadership of society president W. Howard Adams, the 1859 Jail, Marshal's Home and Museum opened to the public June 14, 1959, in the building's one hundredth year. The one-room schoolhouse used for ninety years on the William Bullitt Howard farm near Lee's Summit, Missouri, was later saved and relocated to the site for preservation and interpretation. The restored structures and period rooms are furnished through the acquisition of significant Jackson County–related artifacts from the late nineteenth century.

Membership grew from 700 in 1958 to 2,351 a decade later. During this period, the society acquired the John B. Wornall House on the one hundredth anniversary of the Battle of Westport (an event significant to that site's history) in October 1964. Although the home was open by 1969 for "under restoration" tours, it took another three years of research, planning, fundraising and restoration before the historic house museum opened to the public in September 1972.

The society's Archives and Research Library outgrew temporary quarters in the basement of the Harry S Truman Presidential Museum and Library and relocated in 1973 to a space in the historic Jackson County Courthouse on Independence Square. In 2003, the JCHS partnered with Jackson County Parks and Recreation to assume operational control of the Harry S Truman Office and Courtroom down the hall.

A growing audience makes use of the historical society's products, services, sites and programs. For instance, in 1972 the JCHS archives served about one hundred people annually. Since 2000, they consistently track more than 3,500 contacts and accept more than one hundred collection donations *yearly*. Then, too, are the thousands of museum tours, educational programs, publications, etc.

Today, JCHS is moving into the twenty-first century with technology that will share information about its collections with a worldwide audience.

JACKSON COUNTY HISTORICAL SOCIETY

How do they do it? A productive staff and Board of Directors, faithful volunteers, membership revenues and generous monetary gifts of all sizes help the nonprofit organization vigorously pursue its worthy mission. And tax-deductible contributions to permanent endowment funds are solicited for the long-term viability of this institution with countywide scope.

Support your local historical, nonprofit historical organizations that are dedicated to preserving *your* past for the future!

INDEX

ABOUT THE AUTHOR

D avid W. Jackson received a BS magna cum laude in historic preservation, archives studies. He is founder of the Orderly Pack Rat, a historical research and consulting service. Since 2000, Jackson, as director of Archives and Education for the Jackson County (Missouri) Historical Society, has served as editor of the nonprofit organization's scholarly *JOURNAL*; administers its archives operations; services patron requests through its research library; manages its bookshop; updates its website; coordinates a volunteer program; presents on behalf of its Speakers' Bureau; contributes regular, local history–related articles to area newspapers; and has written and directed the publishing of several products through the society's imprint (available at http://www.jchs.org). The Orderly Pack Rat (http://www.orderlypackrat.com) published Jackson's first book, *Direct Your Letters to San Jose: The California Gold Rush Letters of James and David Lee Campbell, 1849–1852* (2000), and subsequent *Recipes of Our Past: Morsels from Our Grandmothers' Recipe Boxes* (2005).